A PORTRAIT OF JAPAN

A PORTRAIT
OF JAPAN

Laurens van der Post

Photographs by Burt Glinn

William Morrow & Company, Inc., New York 1968

To Margaret Glinn
and Ingaret Giffard

Text copyright © 1968 by Laurens van der Post.

Photographic layout design by Tony Lane.

The author and the photographer wish to express their gratitude to Mr. Harry Sions, and to Mr. Frank Zachary, Mr. Lou Mercier, and the late Mr. Ted Patrick of *Holiday* magazine for commissioning them for the original assignment out of which the present work has been developed.

A different version of this material appeared in *Holiday* magazine under the title "Japan: Journey Through a Floating World."

Library of Congress Catalog Card Number 68-21031.

Contents

I

Return to Japan

The journey to Japan took me first to its head, Tokyo, then to its heart, Kyoto, and only after that to its body. It may well have been better the other way round. One cannot really improve on history in these matters, for history in some intangible fashion prepares one's understanding as can nothing else. The historic approach would have been from the south by sea, landing far from Tokyo at one of the ports of Kyushu, the southernmost of the four main islands of Japan. That is the direction from which the Portuguese, the first Europeans to discover Japan, came in 1542, and for nearly four centuries the seaway opened by the Portuguese remained the main route between the West and Japan. What is more, that, too, may have been the way the Japanese, or at least the subtle Yamato core of their race, so mysterious and remote in its origin, came to their land in some dim stone-age day. But time and distance, those terrible enemies of mortal intentions, joined to compel me to do the 1960 journey by air.

I had only one consolation. As these misgivings assailed me in a jet aeroplane, forty thousand feet up in a Bible-black night and approaching Tokyo at a speed of over 500 miles an hour, I reminded myself that once, many years before, I had followed history to Japan in a way that few people of my generation had done.

Japan was the first country I had known outside Africa. In 1926, just before Emperor Hirohito began his fateful reign, I sailed for Japan in a Japanese ship, the *Canada Maru*. I sailed from Durban, the chief port on that part of the southeast coast of Africa which the great and terrible Vasco da Gama christened Natal when he first set eyes on it on Christmas Day, 1497, during his voyage of discovery to India. The *Canada Maru* by chance followed faithfully in the Portuguese wake: north up the coast of Africa, by Lourenço Marques, Sofala and Mombasa, where it anchored almost within a pebble's throw of the coral-pink walls of the fort built to safeguard their communications by the Portuguese out of stone brought as ballast in their little ships from Lisbon. The *Canada Maru* then sailed on eastwards to the islands of cloves and cinnamon, Zanzibar, Pemba and Ceylon, through the purple straits of Malacca, where the dark jungle feathered with palm steps down to the sea. Skilfully evading the eye of a typhoon off the coast of the island which the Portuguese call Formosa, or The Beautiful, the *Canada Maru,* many weeks after leaving Port Natal, brought us to anchor in the roadstead of the straits of Shimonoseki at the entrance to the Inland Sea of Japan. It was then slightly more than two generations after Commodore Perry's black ships had forced Japan to abandon its determined policy of isolation and to open itself to commerce and intercourse with Europe and America.

In 1926 the impact on my innocent senses of a civilisation so unique and so utterly unlike anything I had encountered before was overwhelming. In those first few moments I came near to realizing the effect Japan must have had on the early Portuguese. Growing up as I had in the interior of Africa, among primitive peoples of all kinds, I had never been predisposed to believe that the European way was the only way of living. Nor did I seem to have any colour prejudice: that was something that just happened to be left out of me. As a result I have always found the different colours and moulds in which the races of the world have been fashioned to be one of the most attractive and endearing facts of life on earth, and to this day I know of nothing more exciting than to discover a new idiom of beauty in a totally different race. The long voyage to Japan in the *Canada Maru,* in which my friend, William Plomer, and I were the only persons not Japanese, had quietly rendered another such idiom within my grasp.

I remember that our arrival was in early autumn. The harbour town was gay with crowds gathered for a great festival. All the women without exception still wore kimonos, and most of the men, too, the oldest officials among them walking about with immense dignity in haori and hakama, those long silk ceremonial clothes of the male in old Japan, with the wearer's family crest punctilliously printed in five places on the upper garment: on each sleeve, each breast and the back of the neck. Watching them gathering round a professional storyteller, with the clothes, face and beard of a Chinese scholar, and listening absorbed to one of the countless legends of their long, rich and dramatic past, I found myself deeply moved.

When at last the clear sun of the autumn day disappeared and the lights, soft in paper lanterns or glowing behind paper walls, were lit against a sky of ink, we climbed up an alley to an ancient wooden inn set among the trees on the mountainside overlooking the narrow strait. Suddenly above the murmur of the gay, soft-spoken crowd we heard first the nostalgic notes of a tune vibrating like a sensitive nerve on a Japanese guitar, and then another bubbling like a fountain out of a bamboo flute. I thought I had never met so attractive a people or encountered such an enchanting world.

From there we made our way across the Inland Sea to Kobe and on to Nara, Kyoto, Arashiyama, by many a famous shrine, temple and hallowed wayside place, until we reached the modern capital, Tokyo. There were also many moments when I had glimpses of the world of mills, factories and pinnacles of glass and steel. But the overriding impression was that of a world unique, rich and civilised in its own pagan right. I was not there long, and when the time came to leave I was nearly heartbroken. I comforted myself on the long voyage home (this time alone and the only European in the ship) by working at my

Japanese and the difficult art of writing it in Chinese characters. When I landed once again in Africa, for the first time in my life my native continent did not seem enough. Suddenly I understood why we had been called "red barbarians" and "foreign devils" when we broke into the East.

I did not see Japan again for nearly a quarter of a century. For years the beautiful experience seemed irrelevant to the main pattern of my life, as if it had been inflicted on me merely as a healthy irritant to my spirit. Then came the return.

After the fall of Singapore, in 1942, I was sent to Java. When Malaya fell, Java was evacuated. Our own troops left, as well as the Dutch government, but I remained behind with some guerrilla forces to contain as many Japanese troops as possible. I took up a position on the top of a vast mountain in the interior of Java called The Peak of an Arrow, and early one morning, carrying no arms whatsoever, with my pockets crammed with medicines for my forward guards on the saddle of the volcanic hill, I suddenly saw Japanese soldiers, armed to the teeth, dropping out of the trees all round me. I had been betrayed by a deserting Chinese servant and our small force had been surrounded by the Japanese during the night. A Japanese lieutenant shrieked an order, a platoon of Japanese fixed bayonets and then, led by the lieutenant, charged straight at me, moving in a closing circle. There was no chance of escape. No chance of anything but certain death for all of us. I held up my hand—and then, out of the irrelevant past, came the relevant word. There are many degrees of polite speech in Japanese. The politest form of all came unbidden to my tongue, although I had not spoken Japanese for sixteen years. I called out a Japanese phrase which can only be translated idiomatically as: "Would you please be so kind as to condescend to wait an honourable moment?"

The advancing soldiers stopped dead. They had expected rifle and machine-gun fire, mortars and hand grenades, certainly not the highest degree of politeness in Japanese. Politeness and courtesy go very deep in the Japanese character. They are never mere ceremoniousness or perfunctory form. Amazed, the officer beat back his men. Profoundly puzzled, he walked up to me, pushed the point of his sword into my navel and asked, "Was that Japanese you spoke?"

I said, "Yes."

He asked, "Where did you learn Japanese?"

I replied, "In Japan."

"You have been to Japan!" he exclaimed, drawing his breath in sharply between his front teeth as the Japanese do when amazed or deeply moved, and making the sound which the uncharitable Pierre Loti compared to a viper's hiss.

And so, by a seeming miracle, my life was saved. And the miracle continued. Unlike others who were bayonetted or beheaded when captured, my life was spared. Even at field headquarters, where I was condemned to be executed for having committed the worst of crimes in the Japanese military mind—"indulging a spirit of wilfulness by carrying on the war against the Imperial Japanese Army after the Allied High Command had surrendered"—the sentence was never carried out. After several months I was released from solitary confinement into the comparative freedom of a prisoner-of-war camp. There for three years I endured the darkest and most negative expressions of the Japanese character, and I emerged from prison, like thousands of others, very near the end of my physical resources. Yet in that period I had managed somehow to go on with my study and practice of Japanese and Japanese writing. I felt no bitterness about the experience, only relief that we all had helped to save the world, ourselves and the Japanese from themselves.

After the war was over, it looked again as if my life had done with Japan. I was once more profoundly preoccupied with Africa, yet I was often aware of a feeling that I could not close my account with Japan after those two conflicting encounters. The feeling became so insistent that in the end I had to come back once again. And now with the brutal abruptness of air travel, thirty hours after leaving London I was in Tokyo. What would I find and what would I feel? More immediately, what would Tokyo be like—now?

Tokyo was an enigma. It surely must be one of the most afflicted cities in the world. As Japanese cities go, it is not old. The first fortress was built in

1457 to control the arrogant nobility of the region; before that it was only an obscure village on the flats, among the reeds, wild geese, and duck of the marshes of Musashi—one of Japan's few really great plains. The plain indeed was so wide that it moved an ancient poet to sing:

"Musashino wa	"On the wide Plain
Tsuki no irukeba	Of Musashi
Yama mo nashi	With no hills at all,
Kusa yori idete	The moon rises
Kusa ni koso ire"	and sets in a sea of grass"

But Tokyo's real fame dates only from 1603, when the formidable Tokugawa Ieyasu became shogun, overlord and master of Japan, and established himself there. In 1868 the seal was permanently set on its importance, after the overthrow of the last shogun and the removal of the Imperial Capital to Tokyo from Kyoto. Its name was changed then from Yedo to Tokyo, or Eastern Capital. But in that short period, it had developed hand in hand with disaster.

First of all there had been the fires which in a city of houses of wood and paper, and narrow streets, turned it time and again into its own funeral pyre. No one can read the history of Japan without grim wonder at the devastation caused by fires everywhere in the country, and the apparent inability of a nation, otherwise so inventive and ingenious, to evolve a system of town-planning capable of preventing them. In fact, there is hardly a town, temple, shrine, or village of note in the entire country that has not been burned down at least once, and many several times.

It is true that the Japanese have founded a system of fire watchers and fire fighters who to this day are perhaps the most adroit and best-trained firemen in the world. But that is rather like locking the stable door after the horse has bolted. In old Yedo itself fires were so numerous that fires all over Japan were nicknamed *"Yedo no Hano* [Flowers of Yedo]." So devastating were they that the Japanese evolved a distinctive language to differentiate between fires, with special terms for an incendiary fire, a fire shared with many others, a fire burning to its end, and so on right down to a special word for the visit of condolence paid to a victim of fire. One of the greatest fires in Tokyo was that of 1657 when over half the city was destroyed and over 107,000 people were burned to death, but there had been others before relatively as great, like the fire of 1601. In 1772 there was another equally devastating, and all the while, particularly in the winter, the sky over the city every night was red with lesser flames.

Sometimes the fire followed in the wake of shattering earthquakes. There are, the Japanese say, four great terrors in life: earthquakes, fire, thunder, and father. Yet of these there can be no doubt that the earthquake is the greatest. Statistics say that there are every year more than two thousand earthquakes in Japan, and though most of them happily are light, no one knows, when the earth begins to flap underneath his feet like the skin of a dog shaking the water out of its coat, where the sinister rhythm will end. Whenever that happens, the Japanese say that the great subterranean fish on which their world rests is waking up and beginning to wriggle about. In this way the city was wrecked by a great earthquake in 1855, and the book *Ansei Kembun Shi,* which describes the horror in detail with the most realistic and skilful illustrations, is one of the most gruesome records of disaster I know. Then, of course, there was the earthquake of 1923, one of the most violent on world record. It shook Tokyo as a terrier does a rat, at noon when all the luncheon fires in the city were lit, and within a few seconds the city was ablaze from end to end.

I was there originally barely three years after the disaster. Everyone still had an earthquake story. I was shown an open space to which forty thousand people had fled with their belongings. These were soon set on fire by the sparks flying "like swarms of burning bees" from the vast city in flames. Thirty thousand persons were burned to death. One of the trapped areas was the Yoshiwara, the immense gold, tinsel, silk and flower-and-willow world of the fifty thousand prostitutes of the city. I saw a tranquil canal on the edge of this brothel quarter

Page 17 Kabuki actor Kanzaburo Toshi wearing lion make-up; 18 Wedding couple pose for portrait after the Shinto ceremony; 19 A camera fan at the springtime Jidai Festival; 20–21 Workers at the IHI Shipbuilding Yard, where they are constructing the world's largest tanker—276,000 tons; 22 A scene from a Music Hall revue in Tokyo; 23 A woman bundled up against the Takayama winter; 24–25 A fog-bound boat on the Inland Sea, near Onomichi; 26 A family on a carnival aeroplane ride in the midst of the cherry blossoms of Nara; 27 Terraced fields near Uwajima; 28 Two moods, two faces, at a festival in Nikko.

and was told that its surface had been thick with the oil from the bodies of the painted women who, burning, hurled themselves into the boiling water. I was told, too, of people wandering dazed through a field nearby who saw some strange "grass" growing out of the earth. Examining it, they found it was a woman's long black hair. They discovered a witness of the tragedy who said that it was the hair of a mother who saw her child disappearing into a crack which had opened in the earth at her feet. She had jumped to save her child, and as she jumped the crack closed and held her hair in its grip.

After the earthquake came a tidal wave which swallowed up thousands of bodies on the shores of Tokyo Bay. Yet there, only three years afterwards, the city was completely rebuilt and I saw no trace of disaster.

First to rise from the ashes was the Yoshiwara. It repeated the astonishing performance in 1945 after Tokyo had been destroyed by bombing, a new experience even in its long record of disasters. The respectable Japanese to this day have not quite recovered from this shock to their sense of propriety. Between March and May, 1945, carpet bombing by the United States Air Forces flattened the capital, set it on fire repeatedly and claimed more victims than did the atom bomb on Hiroshima. The Japanese military did their best to minimize the damage and destroy the statistical evidence. Officially only 137,000 people were killed and 767,000 out of 1,377,000 houses totally destroyed; unofficially 197,000 people were killed and 2,862,000 wounded. After such a blow to the pride of a people who in their long history had neither been invaded nor defeated and to whom self-honour matters more than anything else, how could they have had the heart, or the means, to rebuild as before?

II

Tokyo by Day

The answers were not immediately available there in my jet plane in the dark over the capital, nor on the way from the plane to the terminal in a city at dead of night. I was aware only of an impression of profound change since my visit many years ago. Authority seemed to sit far more humbly and lightly on officialdom. Before the war every official in uniform regarded himself as the representative of his emperor and behaved accordingly. Now all that appeared gone, and the customs, medical and immigration inspectors, who had once examined foreigners as if they were notorious enemy agents, dealt with me with despatch and the utmost courtesy. Again I had found it impossible to arrange hotel accommodation by cable. But on arrival an official immediately took over my problems, went to one of those pillar-box telephones that nowadays are always within easy reach of the public everywhere, and soon I was riding in one of the smoothest of buses on my way to an hotel in the heart of the city. Before the war the telephone was handled by the Japanese almost as if it were an instrument of the devil. Now Japan, I was to find, was as telephone conscious as America, and in Tokyo anyway its system as efficient as the Swiss.

I discovered my hotel was the most modern in Tokyo and had been opened only a month before. From the outside it was an anonymous functional structure of concrete and steel; it might have been anywhere in the world—had the new

Japan conformed utterly to the proliferation of the soap-box cell which passes for architecture in the world today? But alone in my room, I was interested to see that even the planner of this hotel had not forgotten his basic Japanese values. My room was very small, barely twelve feet by nine feet, conforming to the ancient unit of the *tatami,* the straw mats, which defined the smallest area (circa 72 by 37 inches) and multiplications of it in which a grown man can sit, work and sleep.

The Japanese had come to their own terms with electricity, too, and used it skilfully. Behind harvest-gold panelling it was so arranged that the light was everywhere, the room without shadows, and yet it was impossible to detect a single highlight. Finally, there was a flower vase on my table. It was not full of flowers; there was a single rose in it. The "Eminent Professor of Flower Arrangement," who came each day to do the flowers in the hotel and whom I was to meet, had fixed the rose in the vase at a subtle angle as if it were bowing politely to the wind of change blowing in the mind of Japan.

I had to wait until daylight for the answers to the questions posed over the airport in the dark the night before, and then it took several days before I could give them shape. I walked along the great and most popular street of Tokyo, the Ginza, or the Silver Place, named three and a half centuries ago when the shoguns minted their coin there. At first I had no eyes for the city because of the people. I thought that such a density and concentration of human beings was purely local and due to some abnormal attraction in the vicinity. I expected at any moment to break out of the swarms of people and find some less congested quarter. But before long I discovered that the apparently abnormal was the normal. Up and down, at every street corner where I paused, I saw swollen tributaries of humanity augmenting the flood sweeping me along. Everywhere I went the city seemed to be ceaselessly boiling and bubbling with human beings. Perhaps only statistics can carry conviction. The mayor of Tokyo, who, far from being proud of the mere size of his city, was worried to death as to how he was to house, transport and provide sanitation and sewage for his soaring population, told me that the next census would show Tokyo to have nine and a half million people living in it and its suburbs. This number was annually increased, he said, by over 300,000. Every day buses, streetcars, steam and electric trains, some 370,000 private cars and 18,000 taxis transported over two million persons between the suburbs and their places of work in the city proper. At the end of the day they reversed the process. Also, from dawn to midnight, their wives, children, country cousins and visitors in their myriads shuttled in and out of the dark stations and subways to shop and amuse themselves in a thousand and one ways.

In the country itself, so great is the Japanese gift for making little seem much, one forgets how grossly overpopulated Japan is. About the size of California, its population totals over ninety-three million. Since only 16 per cent of the earth is cultivable, the density of population on the basis of arable land available reaches the appalling figure of 1,700 per square kilometre—the highest on earth. At the same time the population increases at the rate of over 700,000 a year, nearly half of whom insist upon being absorbed into Tokyo. In Tokyo certainly one is not allowed to forget for a moment that almost intolerable pressure of numbers. Even in these great white concrete office blocks that have arisen gleaming out of the ashes of war in business quarters like the Maranouchi, the sense of pressure pursues one, and I was amazed at the numbers of people working within them and the minute ration of space allotted to each.

As bewildering as the numbers was the outward appearance of the crowd. I looked in vain for some master fashion in their dress. Outwardly all was mixture and confusion. The kimono, except for a few elderly ladies and a few little girls, seems to have vanished. In the whole length of the Ginza I saw only one elderly gentleman in a kimono and he spoilt the effect by swinging a walking stick like a retired brigadier and scowling at me fiercely from underneath a bowler which might have come straight from the City of London. For the rest, I encountered all conceivable variations of Western dress. The women were the most bewildering. They wore anything from the latest fashions of Paris, London, or New York down to jeans and even shorts. Yet on the whole they wore them well, particularly the young girls, and that, too, was something new. Something has happened to their figures, too, for they are taller and straighter than their predecessors. All the old Japanese hands used to swear over their whisky sours and gin slings that Japanese women looked attractive only in kimonos. It was true that the kimono, unfortunately, completely hid the lines of their breasts, but then it also covered up their short, often sabre-shaped legs and exaggerated hips. And above all, the kimono set off the great glory of the Japanese woman, her graceful Victorian shoulders and elegant neck so finely joined to a shapely head and a face, wide-eyed, small and white under her heavy pile of black hair.

But now the young women in Tokyo wore their infinite variations of Western dress as if to the manner born. Vanished, too, was the tradition of getting a skilled hairdresser once every two months to arrange their hair until it rose like a model of some lacquered pagoda over their brows, and forced them to sleep at night not on a pillow but with their necks on a narrow trestle to prevent the precious pile from becoming disarrayed. Now their hair was cut, waved, wind-swept in the several ways prescribed for young women in American fashion magazines; or, if they wore it long, it fell straight over back and shoulders, as uninhibited as any artist's model.

Where I did see an intrusion of the dress of the past, it was because of some function or special occasion. I met an itinerant flute player with his head still in his traditional basket as if hiding, ostrich-like, from the urgent present; two Buddhist nuns with shaven heads and faces shining with a serenity beyond time and space; what seemed to be a mediaeval samurai but was a man advertising a new brand of whisky, followed by a procession of priests who suddenly appeared at a crossroad moving slowly towards a wooden shrine standing behind a fringe of ancient pines imprisoned between rigid concrete buildings. The priests were dressed in spotless white robes that fell to their ankles, with socks and straw sandals, black-lacquer hats and capes of virgin gold silk over their shoulders. Behind them came a group of young men in short frocks of dark- and light-blue checks, in stockinged legs and wooden sandals and with kerchiefs on their heads; they were carrying with exalted expressions a palanquin of unstained wood from whose struts fluttered, like the wings of butterflies, papers bearing prayers of the devout.

All traffic came to a standstill as the procession passed. Toyopets and Datsuns (the Fords and Hillmans of Japan), the reeling streetcars, the motorcyclists in crash helmets, the cyclists with white masks of gauze, like surgeons, over mouth and nose to protect them from contagious dust, the platoon of men disguised as insects prancing down the street to advertise a patent compound food, school-boys in uniform hurrying to school, firemen in uniform, postmen in uniform, a bearded Sikh or two, some Chinese, a party of American servicemen, Pakistanis in black astrakhan hats, Hindus in white nightshirts, a group of blonde Norwegian girls in shoulderless dresses, and wave upon wave of Japanese clerks and businessmen in all manner of European clothes—all stopped like a well-drilled military formation on a single command to let this vision of the past safely through. Then with its passing the traffic of vehicles and humanity roared abruptly into movement again like water hastening to find the main stream at the foot of an abysmal fall.

But what brought Japan in such terrible profusion to Tokyo? Work, first of all. In and around Tokyo alone there are over 50,000 factories trying to manufacture the sort of exports which will give Japan the foreign exchange to buy the food that it cannot grow for its excess millions. It is not hard to detect—behind the almost desperate ingenuity, invention and sustained energy with which Tokyo's millions set about their tasks—the silent, stifling pressure of the expanding millions which makes production a matter of life and death. The skill and inventiveness of the Japanese manufacturer, judging by what I saw in shops, factories and shipyards, are truly stupendous.

In my hotel American, Australian, English, Swiss and Italian businessmen tried to persuade me that the whole of Japanese industry is nothing but a swindle and a gigantic cribbing of others' inventions and industrial designs. It is an old story and one that no doubt was largely true in the modern beginning. When I was first in Japan, the charges of dishonesty in copying foreign goods and then putting them on the world market as original merchandise were common complaints against Japanese manufacturers and no doubt rooted to some extent in reality.

One of the troubles was that in the traditional pattern of Japanese society the merchant and trader were always a degraded class. First came the samurai, the warriors—gentry or squires of whom the daimyo, the so-called great names, were the leaders. Utter scorn for money and money-making was one of the few fundamentals in the samurai's simple code of honour. Below the samurai came the peasantry, then the artisans and last of all the tradesmen. As a result, commercial morality became as degraded as the commercial class itself. For two generations it affected Japanese commerce like a disease, and traces of the sickness persist to this day. But my impression is that the Japanese manufacturer on the whole, like the Quaker merchant of the seventeenth century, has discovered that honesty as policy pays. Certainly he has mastered the technique of scientific research and its application in industry to such an extent that he is producing now on his own original lines. In this he has been abetted not only by the terrible spur of overpopulation but also by the inborn skill, discipline and devotion of the Japanese artisans, craftsmen and workers. I know of no other country in the world in which skill comes so naturally as to these men. Even the cheapest things produced in Japan tend to be objects of care and beauty and seem to have passed through the imagination of a craftsman. Added is the fact that monotony has no terrors for the Japanese worker. Unlike his Western counterpart whose initiative is soon drained, if not utterly exhausted, by routine, the Japanese finds a significant freedom in it. Throughout the ages he has been accustomed to do only one thing in life and in the process to transmit what he has mastered to his sons, who in turn pass on the skill to *their* sons, and so on, until the aptitude for the craft has become second nature. In this, too, he may be helped by the Buddhist elements of his philosophy and the sacred exercises whereby he importunes the forces of creation with prolonged repetition of a single holy phrase of Mantra, until the repetition empties his mind of all other considerations and leaves it open to the reincarnative powers of the

Master. Even in Tokyo's many pachinkos, or pin-table saloons, where he will stand in queues waiting for his turn after work, he gives one the impression that it is the monotony of the act of playing over and over again with the same little ball aimed at the same little hole which fascinates and relaxes him, as if the game were not just a gamble but a way of acting out a Mantra of fortune before the Lord Buddha. The fact that he is unsuccessful 999 times out of a thousand merely seems to confirm rather than deny his belief.

Then the Japanese is the least egotistical of workers. He is from birth conditioned to feel, think, imagine and apply himself to the whole rather than the individual part, first the family, then the clan, then the community and so on to the nation. Alone he may appear to lack individuality and to be of mediocre capacity. But as a member of a team or a group he is outstanding and singularly gifted. Deeper still is his almost extrasensory perception of the nature of the material with which he works. There below the Western man in him, below the Buddhist, the Korean and Chinese levels in his spirit, is the instinctive Shinto sense of communion with nature. As a result he tends to work with reverence for the intrinsic nature of the material in his hand. Watch him painting the Chinese characters for the name of a teahouse on a paper lantern, or patiently trimming for hours the same ornamental shrub in a garden, or lacquering a rice bowl or assembling a hi-fi radio or welding the plates of a ship; his expression is that of a man whose entire personality is participating in the work.

Such absolute commitment to the task is rare in the modern world. At one time the Japanese had a special word for expressing the mystique of their relationship with the things they fashioned according to some image of their spirit. It is that strange, ancient, untranslatable word *maru,* which today is joined only to the names of merchant ships. But previously the samurai tagged it onto the name he gave his sword, the daimyo to his castle, the priest to his symbolic flail, and the musician to his instrument. Though the custom has contracted, the state of mind that produced it persists.

While in Japan I saw a photograph of workers assembled in their factory, which was about to be equipped with new machinery. They were there to thank the old machine before it was scrapped for its faithful service, and the photograph showed them bowing to it in an act of profound gratitude.

All in all, these things make the Japanese potentially the most skilled and original industrial nation of our time. Indeed, had they raw materials and physical resources as they have imagination, skill and will, they would sweep the markets of the world.

Of course there is a negative aspect to this. Somewhere along the line of advance a price has to be paid for it, and as a rule it is paid for by the individual. Surrounded by so many millions, faced with such a vast and unwanted increase of population, forced from birth to circumscribe and deny his own particular self, and predisposed to subordinate himself to an almost mystical identification with the great impersonal forces of nature and time, the individual is always in peril of feeling that he is unimportant. As a result, he tends to take his own life. In Tokyo alone on the average five suicides take place each day. For the whole country the annual rate may be the highest in the world, twenty-four out of every hundred thousand. Not all the suicides have the same causes, but it is significant that in most cases they are attributed to a phenomenon called *ensei*—weariness of living.

But to return to the work of the millions who find it possible to accept the bondage of their society so implicitly that it becomes another kind of freedom.

The Ginza, the main street of Tokyo, is a vast exhibition, daily revised, of the products of labour. It is astonishing what one finds on display here from both the ancient world and the new. Side by side with a Chinese chemist's shop displaying cures for the ills and curses of the flesh—all the ingredients of the witches' brew in *Macbeth* and more—stands a soaring concrete block filled from ground floor to roof garden with the latest medicines and drugs from aureomycin to penicillin, the work of the Institute of Scientific Research and corporate bodies: typical examples of the Japanese genius for group endeavour. Next to a modest wooden shop selling *bonsai*, those two-hundred-year-old dwarf trees in pots, mysteriously made to resemble in every detail (except size)

the fifteen-hundred-year-old giants that one sees on the skyline of Japan's indigenous forests, soars a department store crammed with the latest products of
the modern world.

They really deserve a chapter to themselves, these department stores of
Japan. They are, of course, at their most impressive in Tokyo, Osaka and the
bigger Japanese cities. But there is not a town of note where they do not exist,
and they draw the nation to them as if to some temple of the commercial world.
I mingled with the Japanese crowds in many of them all over the country and
was convinced that the people went not merely to buy but to satisfy their innate
and all-important *Gemütlichkeit* and, all together, to sample visually the character and nature of a feverishly changing modern world. These department
stores did not ignore the products of the thousands of small factories still dedicated to the traditional arts and crafts of Japan, but their preference clearly was
for the new. They seemed to me to contain everything important produced not
only in Japan but also in the whole world.

In the bookshops, for instance, I found the books of all the world displayed,
not just the more important Japanese, Chinese and European books, but also
the Indian, Arabic and even rare Sanskrit and Tantric tomes. It would be a great
mistake to suppose that the new Japan is interested only in the West. It seemed
to me open wide to all countries. Significantly this section of the department
store was always most crowded, and both the crowds and the books available
testified to the profound respect the Japanese have for knowledge and learning.
The *sensei,* the teacher, is perhaps the most venerated person in the whole
country. For instance, I myself shall never forget the manner in which the
little Japanese girl in the lift at the hotel asked me whether I too was a *sensei.*
When I asked why she thought I might be one, she pointed at the book in my
hand and said with an envy that humbled me, "Because books seem to be your
home."

Yet few of the people in the crowds ever bought a book at all. Many were
students who are too poor to pay for the books they need. They go daily to
one of the many bookshops in Tokyo and stand there for hours, the relevant

text in hand, studying for their exams. They may do this freely, since by tradition you can read a book in a Japanese bookshop for as long as you like, provided you do not sit down.

All the other departments were equally well stocked. The food floor sold anything from caviar and *pâté de foie gras* and edible seaweed to the cured cockroaches powdered for sprinkling on rice and reputed to be of great dietetic value. The clothing sections sold anything from plus-fours for the new-rich, who have taken to golf on their expense accounts, to blazing kimonos for geisha. In the bigger department stores, in fact, one can buy anything from real estate to glass-bottomed yachts. Most of them, too, have their own stockbroking and jobbing sections, and in one I saw Vitamin-C injections being administered over the counter by a pretty girl with a hypodermic syringe to customers for a couple of yen a time.

Outside, both stores and shops have screeds carrying large Chinese characters advertising their products. In the sky red balloons trail pennants of similar characters exhorting the streams of humanity below to buy someone's toffee, beer, candy, toothpaste, patent medicine, sake or aphrodisiac. Up there in the blue the red balloons give commercial rivalry a curious warlike look, and even had I not known a single Chinese ideograph, I would have been provoked and haunted by the sight. By night when the characters are written on paper lanterns and in neon lighting they are especially provocative.

That is another feature of the new world of Japan: it has taken to advertising like a fish to water. One American businessman told me he thought that Japanese magazine advertising was technically and visually the most original and effective he had ever encountered. In this crowded world of material things in which night and day one is beseeched, cajoled, intimidated and tempted to buy, the particular glory is that of the small. The Japanese have always excelled at the small things of life. Their deepest psychological bias inclines them to find the infinite in a grain of sand. So marked is this trend that we Westerners, out of our obsession with the physically imposing, have taunted their artists and philosophers with the slick half-truth that though they may be great in small things, they are small in the great.

I have always divided humanity roughly into two main streams: those who work by expansion and those who work by contraction. The Japanese have a genius for contraction. Just as the *bonsai,* the dwarf pine, is a symbol in ancient Japan of this aspect of the national genius, so today the precision instrument of the modern craftsman is its manifestation. Postwar Japan has translated into modern terms the age-old capacity of the craftsman. As a maker of lenses he rivals the best German craftsmen, of precision instruments the Swiss. More of his cameras and field glasses are sold in the United States than those of any other country, not excepting Germany. In the Far East he has practically eliminated all rivals in the field. His television sets are as good as any in existence and in some ways in advance of them. One of his most successful achievements is the production of his tiny transistor radio. At first he was laughed at for trying to produce commercially so small a thing. He nearly ruined himself financially in the effort. But today ironically those who laughed are foremost in sharing the profits of his success. He has made sets that can receive all Japanese stations and are so minute that they are no bigger than a hearing aid. It took me a long time in my first Pullman to realise that I was not looking at a coach full of deaf businessmen from Osaka but at people plugged in to a broadcast of sumo, the traditional wrestling tournament being held in Tokyo!

In all these fields the thought of making something smaller, neater, more precise seems to excite the Japanese imagination as nothing else does. And as a nation he does not indulge in thought for thought's sake as the European intellectual tends to do. Indeed, that is a luxury he suspects instinctively to be an evasion of reality. The idea, for him, is there to be lived, if necessary to be died for.

Yet he has not ignored the great. The progress of Japanese heavy industry since the war has been phenomenal, thanks as much to American generosity as to native capacity. The shipbuilding yards, like those of Nagasaki, which enabled Japan to build in secret the largest battleships the world has ever seen, today turn out some of the biggest tankers afloat. Japan now ranks with the foremost shipbuilding nations in the world, and its big engineering, electrical and even motorcar industries are securing orders and markets all over the world. Of the working millions in Tokyo alone, 26 per cent are engaged in production of the kind I have just outlined, 18 per cent in commerce and 6 per cent in reconstruction and construction.

The achievement of the 6 per cent is perhaps the most impressive of all. When at last I was free to turn from the people to the appearance of the city itself, I had found my answer to the question of the night before. There was no trace left of the disaster of the war. The reconstruction I saw everywhere was a result of pulling down the old to make way for the new. This went on night and day at a steady, continuous rhythm. Everything I had read in advance had prepared me to find the rebuilt area of Tokyo distasteful. It is true that the modern architecture in the capital is not beautiful, but in that respect it is no worse than in most other modern towns I know. Function and work, not beauty and leisure, dominate the mind of the modern architect. Besides, the imagination of the Japanese is not stimulated by the thought of building for industry and commerce, from which his deepest sympathies are withheld. To me it was most interesting to find that when the Japanese builds for a purpose close to his heart, for example in the cause of learning, or where the Emperor still evokes his sense of communion, he produces original and striking results.

The builder in Japan is by tradition and instinct a carpenter. His idiom for centuries has been wood and paper, and no one has used wood in building more beautifully. To this day the feeling of the Japanese builder is for this material, he is aware of its texture and grain, he shapes and polishes its unstained surface until it glows and gleams like amber. And somehow he has come to realise that the modern architect with steel beams and rafters can be a carpenter in another dimension. Frank Lloyd Wright, whose Imperial Hotel is still one of the most remarkable modern buildings in Tokyo, has done as much to make the Japanese imagination aware of this parallel as Japan's native architecture

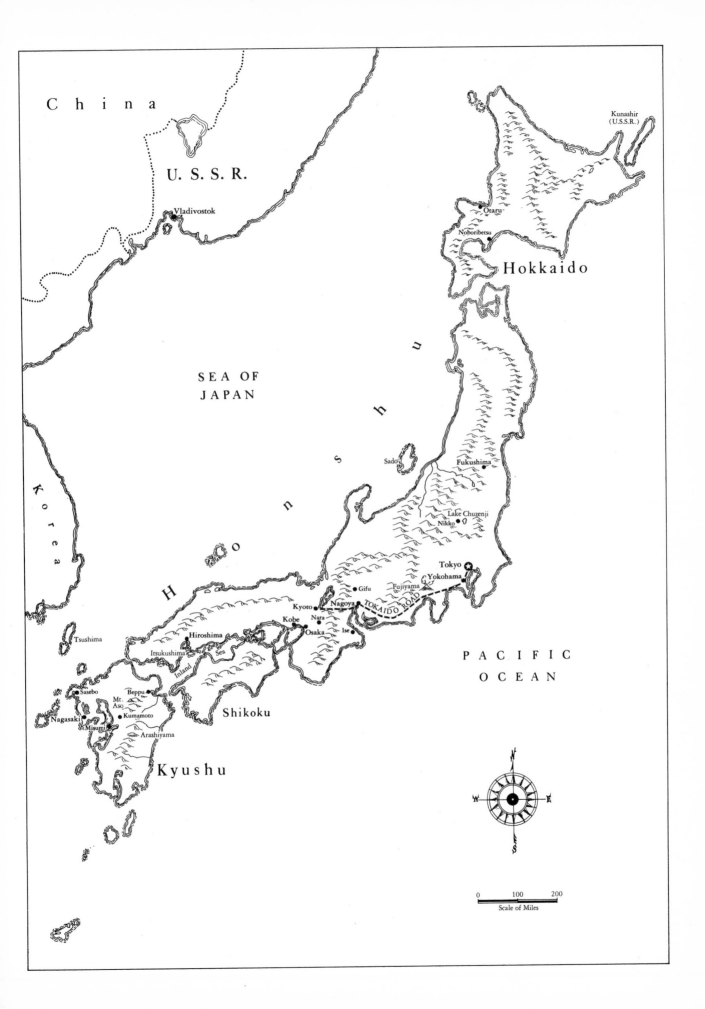

influenced his own inspiring conception of building. The Ehime Convention Hall, the Kanagawa Library, the Leisure Centre at Sendai University, the Memorial Hall of Kanto-Gakuin University, the Hasshokan Inn at Navoya, where I spent a night of rest, peace and beauty, and even the railway station at Kyoto seem to me remarkable evidence of this trend. This tendency would be even more marked if the Japanese was not withheld by his instinctive dislike of show. Profoundly retrospective at heart, he is the least exhibitionist of men. The Buddhist in him despises the world of appearances or, as he puts it, "the world of floating things." His Shinto identification with nature and his sense of the animate within the inanimate make the abstractions on which so much in the modern world depends repellent to him. So the elements of the provisional and the incongruous in his cities of commerce worry him less than they would us. In a sense they have all been discounted in advance because at heart there is the *a priori* assumption that commerce is not a dignified occupation.

This does not mean that a Japanese has not his own fastidious commitment to beauty and proportion. Like the fabulous works of art hidden in the darkened storerooms of his temples and shrines and brought out for exhibition perhaps only once a year, his home and his life within the home are hidden from the outside world. To discover this one has to go to the thousands of wood-and-paper villas, the far-flung bundles of villages tied together and to the capital by the bright ribbons of steel railways: all this constitutes the scattered principality of Tokyo. Seek out your Japanese in miniature gardens behind neat hedges or wooden walls fringed with pines, and go to sit facing him as he squats on his *zabuton* (a flat, square seating cushion on the *tatami,* beautiful, tightly fitting yellow mats of plaited straw that serve as carpet to his room), while his womenfolk wait on him and his guests as if they were the lords of creation. Above all, until you have had a bath with him and his family, devoutly washing the dirt of the world of things from yourself at the end of the day as does even the meanest of coolie and peasant, you will have no idea how fastidious a spirit has been hidden from you in the fevered vulgarity and desperation of the daily round. Unfortunately, few foreigners, even those who have spent many years in Japan, ever penetrate into this other and, in my view, more important world.

In Tokyo itself one gets, perhaps, the clearest impression of the two worlds. Everything represented in our time exists side by side without apparent cohesion or relation. From the Nijubashi, the arched double bridge which spans the moat to the Imperial Palace, looking across the wide open space, one has a superb view of the city's modern skyline. Great office blocks dominate the whole of the horizon. There are no skyscrapers, since respect for Tokyo's earthquake has made the planners limit building to a maximum of nine stories, but a thousand-foot television tower stands like a giant exclamation mark over a graceful and humble shrine and dominates the 146-odd fire-watch towers which are still needed in the capital. Yet at one's back always there is that wide, tranquil moat of gleaming water with swans white as flakes of Antarctic snow merging with their own bright reflections, and behind them rise the grey walls of the Palace. These walls are breath-taking. They are made of enormous blocks of stone, all of different shapes, and yet they have been used so superbly that they rise smoothly without flaw or effort and curve upwards in a movement as graceful and spontaneous as a Mozart melody. All this was possible because of a secret formula which died with the builders. They were so concerned for the future of their master-building that they buried alive in the foundations volunteers from among their workmen to appease the forces of evil and imperfection that might have threatened the purity of design they had in mind. Above the lovely wall are pines with the rheumatism of time deep in their ancient joints. They are twisted and bowed, yet full of the beauty of the suffering of history, and they hide the Palace utterly from view.

It is called a palace, but surely there has never been a palace less like the Western or even the Chinese conception of the word. It is a collection of discreet villas, mostly of wood and paper, scattered all over the vast grounds. Stone was used only for defence in Japan, wood and paper for light and delight at home.

I remembered when first I saw the Palace that I had to get out of our car with my Japanese friend and bow to the walls before we could drive on. Conductors of buses and streetcars, too, in passing, would draw the attention of passengers to the Palace, and at once they would rise to their feet in the swaying vehicle and bow as low as its motion permitted. I could not help wondering how much of that world had survived. For most foreign observers the answer is not in doubt. They say that modern Japan has a split personality. The patter stolen from modern psychology gives this slick observation an appearance of profundity, but I had a hunch that all this was too glib to be true. From what I knew of the Japanese I suspected that the split might not be great. Yet I must confess as I contemplated the incredible, unselective, uncontrolled and gigantic mixture of humanity, fashions, forms of knowledge, religions, superstitions, crazes, products and ways of living that I encountered in Tokyo, I was not at all sure. Nor was my hunch made more certain by my encounter with the young people of Tokyo in the mass.

The population of this city is surely one of the youngest in the world. That is largely due to the fact that the capital is the greatest educational centre in the land. There are seventy-eight universities in Tokyo alone with approximately 320,000 students. There are 980 secondary and over 900 primary schools with a prodigious number of pupils. And since students and pupils all wear uniforms, they are conspicuous in every crowd and scene. The students have a hard time of it. Only one in twenty ever succeeds in getting into the better colleges. Once there they must work extremely hard, and since almost all are poor, they get jobs in their spare time to eke out their pittances from home. They do this by working as guides to foreigners, or as sandwich men, or even by joining in public demonstrations against the government or municipality for a few yen an hour. They also wash dishes or tout for restaurants and night clubs.

The Kanda quarter and the coffeehouses in the new west wards of the city —which the young prefer to the bars and night clubs of the Ginza—are worlds essentially of the eager and the immature, who search, seek, listen and talk all night long about anything from Dostoevski, Marilyn Monroe, political theory, economic practice and Picasso to nuclear fission and the Bolshoi Ballet. For them Japan has no past. The term *avant-guerre* is always on their lips. The phrase is pronounced like a sentence of intellectual death. But it is real praise to label something *après-guerre,* which they have contracted into *apuré.*

Between the two periods is the dark gulf of war.

"What do you feel about the war?" I asked the question of many, and they all said quickly that it was bad, that it must not happen again, and then hastened to change the subject. Consciously they dissociate themselves from it all. Yet in the modern personality, does not that produce another fateful evasion? Can a modern spirit be truly contemporary without looking the war in the face and trying to understand it? These young people seem to believe all they have to do is to disown it. After all, are they not *apuré?*

A certain desperate element of overcompensation inevitably enters their world of *apuré.* And what was most *apuré* when I was in Tokyo was modern Western music, from Britten and Bartók to jazz and rock-and-roll. Most popular of all were French songs, and in café after café I saw the young sitting for hours listening to other young people singing in a language they could not understand. Significant, too, was the strange inner excitement which gripped singers and musicians as they performed in the Western idiom. The rhythm accelerated as the tune progressed, the interpretation became oddly obsessional, energy and passion seized the pianist by his slender wrists and the crew-cut singer by the throat, until the concluding bars flew upwards like an eruption. One could not deny that the young found what looked foreign and disordered from without, dynamic and alive within.

Their games, too, are modern. They go in for skiing, skating, ice hockey, tennis, netball, rowing and above all baseball. For this last the enthusiasm is as great as in the United States. Undergraduates, complete with organised supporters and cheerleaders, draw as great crowds as skilled professional teams. When first-class teams meet on either amateur or professional level there is not a television set that is not tuned in for the broadcast. At the same time universities will continue to send expeditions of students to climb the unclimbed in the Himalayas, explore the heights of the Rockies and even probe the Antarctic.

Yet in spite of the sense of things *apuré,* some games and entertainment of the past have their own nostalgic following. Indeed, sumo, traditional wrestling, which is a game for professionals only and turns out to entertain the public as a kind of geisha in a male dimension, has more than a nostalgic following. The Emperor himself attends the final meetings of the greatest sumo tournaments, and while I was in Tokyo, the decisive tournament produced an atmosphere I have experienced in Britain only on Derby Day. But jujitsu or judo, fencing and archery nowadays seem to draw only the more imaginative and selective among the young. What they lack in numbers they certainly make up for in quality.

One afternoon after a boisterous moment at a baseball stadium of which an old Japanese friend of mine was president, I went to the nearby Yasakuni shrine. It is the shrine where the spirits of all those who died for their country are supposed to reside, and it is said that the palanquins carried to the shrines on the Japanese equivalent of All Souls' Day become so heavy with the spirits of the dead returning for the occasion that their ardent bearers can hardly lift them. While I was in Tokyo someone had written to the newspapers saying that President Eisenhower, who was about to visit the country, must be given the opportunity of visiting this shrine. The letter raised a storm of protests. This was considered to be a dangerous revival of the Shinto presumption which had led to the war, for no particular shrine could claim to house the spirit of the dead sacrificed by homes of different cults, creeds and beliefs in Japan.

Whatever the merits of the hotly debated dispute, I went to the shrine because I wanted to devote some time and thought to a place sacred to the relations of the men I had helped to kill. Accordingly I went with a young student, charming, intelligent and not excessively *apuré*. We walked in the lovely park around the shrine on a tender spring day. We entered through the huge concrete torii, or monumental arch, past a great door adorned with a golden chrysanthemum of sixteen petals, symbol of sun and emperor, and along an imposing avenue until we came to the heart of the shrine, a simple, bare and totally unadorned building of wood. An ex-soldier with wooden leg and begging bowl hobbled on crutches towards us. I was amazed how angry my young Japanese companion became. Had the sight quickened an unconscious awareness of the evasions which I have mentioned? Rather like Macbeth trying to exorcise the ghost of Duncan, he ordered the wreck in faded uniform away. "Don't give him anything," he said to me. "It is against the law. The state has provided for persons like him. He has no right to be here."

However, I insisted on recalling the man and giving him something. I hated his war and the manner in which he had waged it, but I could not help remembering my first visit to the shrine long before the war. Then everyone who came to it first washed his hands at a wayside trough, rinsed his mouth with water and then presented himself to the shrine, bowing low and clapping his hands to attract the attention of the gods, and ending by throwing a handful of coins in a special money-box. Now only the older people did it. The younger ones went there only out of curiosity and looked rather bored and superior.

On our way back we saw a crowd of young people assembled. We joined them and found an archery contest in progress. The archers were all young and of both sexes. They presented themselves to the target in groups of seven. Before shooting their arrows they would remove their shoes, fall on their knees, bow low to it and, arising, arrange themselves sideways to it. Up would come the long bow, an arrow fitted to it, and then the bow would be drawn slowly to its full extent in a continuous, highly stylised movement. The aiming of the arrow in a bow at full stretch would seem to last an age. Then came that lovely swish of silk as the arrow flew. Again down on his knees the archer would go, bowing low, before making his exit. A slender young archer near us told me that hitting the inner target was not so important as the manner in which the archer came to the target, aimed and shot his bolt. It should all be one continuous movement like water gathering on a leaf until it becomes so heavy that the leaf bends and a drop of water falls from it. Only in that way can the arrow be truly shot.

The young men and women of Tokyo constitute a formidable element in the life of the capital and the nation. Perhaps one disquieting aspect of their world is an increasing mistrust of their elders. The young feel that they have a special political mission. At one end there is the extreme left-wing students' union, the Zengakuren, which is too violent even for the foxy Japanese Communist and which played such an infamous role in the demonstrations against the Security Treaty with the United States. At the other end inevitably there are some small right-wing unions for whom the imperial past is still a present. On the credit side is the fact that the great bulk of the Japanese are idealistic, vaguely though eagerly seeking for axioms to build a world wherein everything will be changed for the better: relationships between child and parents, boy and girl, man and society, society and the universe.

As for the schoolchildren, one saw them after school usually, young boys in black uniforms, or young girls, with their black hair and black eyes, wearing neat navy-blue sailor suits and jumpers, out endlessly sightseeing at temple and shrine or touring the countryside. The little boys would always be solemn and full of synthetic dignity; the girls gay, curious and chattering like starlings. People complained that they overcrowded the famous places, buses and trains and were too young to understand what they were shown. But their teachers, the *sensei,* insisted it was the right preparation for life, and that anyway it kept them off the streets.

III

Tokyo by Night

Finally, there is Tokyo at night. As the two million workers withdraw from the centre at the end of the day another world comes alive. Along the Ginza the footlights in thirty or more theatres and 700 bars are switched on. Here a Tokyo which has replaced prewar Shanghai as the most cosmopolitan town in the world caters to every taste in food and entertainment that exists. Suddenly the streets are full of night-club hostesses heavily made up, in short backless evening frocks and high golden heels. They mix with geisha in bright kimonos and lacquered hair strutting like cranes on their high wooden *geta* as they all hasten in their thousands to their work of entertaining the male. My Japanese guidebook told me Japan was poor in raw materials and rich only in manpower. She is richer still in womanpower. One could not believe there were so many young women in the world free to give themselves over to this sort of life. In every bar behind the counter there is not only a barman to serve the customers, but shoulder to bare shoulder a line of young bar hostesses talk to each customer while he does his drinking. There are dance halls so full of young hostesses that as the customers come in they are summoned on a loudspeaker by their special number. There is one theatre wherein a chorus of over ''a hundred nude atomic'' girls dances between the main acts.

I went with a Japanese friend to one night club where the girls first came out of the wings onto a flood-lit stage, then were raised from the floor by a lift, and finally descended from the ceiling in a balloonist's basket. They were there for the purpose of what my Japanese friends called *sturippo;* and indeed once assembled on the stage they began to strip. Stripping, they started to disappear into the wings, teasing the audience with the impression that they would vanish before the full act of revelation. But at the last moment they paused, stark naked, at their several exits while the music of cymbal, saxophone and drum issued a proclamation of strange triumph.

The ingenuity and the desperate search for novelty in bars, cabarets and theatres is astounding. One bar dressed up barmen and hostesses in military uniforms and gave its customers ranks from corporal to field marshal and admiral, according to the money they spent. Nor was this all; in the background was another world of women. Officially, the Yoshiwara brothel quarters have been abolished. But people say there are still in Tokyo 40,000 illegal establishments as well as 80,000 night walkers. Who knows for certain? With all these millions one is inclined to say, wearily, what do another few thousand either way matter?

But somewhere in these vast numbers there is an individual. And what is this individual like? In a fashionable night club to which my Japanese friends took me one of the four hostesses who sat at our table was a Japanese girl from the country, who said she did this to help her parents since they were very poor; another, the daughter of a Japanese father and German mother who was trying to earn money to go to Germany to study music; one was the daughter of a White Russian father and a Japanese mother, earning money to help pay for her brother's university education; the last was a Tokyo girl and all I learned about her was that she tried to get each one of us in turn to take her home. My Japanese friends asked them all if they had a young man of their own. They all shyly said yes, except the hostess who was half Russian. With a touch of un-Japanese bitterness she said, "No one loves me!"

One Sunday evening, getting into the lift of my hotel on the way to my room, I found two men with a slight Japanese girl in a simple silk evening dress between them. It was late and there was no attendant. I turned to ask them which floor was theirs and heard the girl pleading in Japanese for them to let her go. Then I saw that their arms were linked in hers.

I thought they looked British and said in English, "You must excuse me, but do you realise this girl is asking you to let her go?"

"You don't say, old boy," they exclaimed with a pronounced accent, obviously not believing me.

I spoke to the girl in Japanese, and with immense relief she turned to say she was extremely sorry that she appeared to have caused a misunderstanding with the honourable foreign gentlemen. She apologised. It was her fault. In a sense they were not mistaken. She was indeed a prostitute. Only she was a prostitute on every night of the week *except* Sunday. On Sundays, she said with pride, she was herself, slept late, went to the temple, walked in the park to look at the flowers and gardens, in the evening had a bath, changed and then came to the hotel to listen to the French songs, which she loved. So she hoped the honourable gentlemen would understand and excuse her. "In the week," she said, touching her heart with a delicate finger, "I am a machine, but tonight I am *tamako* [jewel]." She stood there, eyes bright, as she pronounced her name.

"Please tell her," the two men said, bowing to her, "we're sorry for our mistake." With that they escorted her out of the lift and back to the hotel entrance.

This world in Tokyo is very largely that of foreigners and visitors. Even some of the most successful night clubs and cabarets are owned and run by Chinese who fled from the austere Communist rule in Shanghai and introduced their expertise in these matters with great profit to themselves. Similarly, some of the finest restaurants in the city are run by Chinese and the Japanese claim that the best food in the world is to be had in these. On a warm night in the streets parallelling the Ginza, the smell of thousands of different dishes being prepared —Chinese and Japanese, Indian, Malay, Dutch and Hungarian, Italian, Russian and French, flavoured with all the spices of the East plus the herbs of Europe— is almost suffocating. But on the whole the Japanese, unless they are out for a feast, dining on an expense account, or just sightseeing, avoid this world. They are a Spartan people and not fond of excess and prefer to amuse themselves less ostentatiously and more economically. They do so in areas like that around the Ueno Station, the Asakusa or the Shinjuku districts, which alone house some two hundred geisha and cabaret establishments and sixty or more cinemas. They have their own select teahouses and restaurants where admission is only by personal introduction from old clients of the establishment. Some of these geisha houses give on the hundreds of canals or stretches of the Sumida River, and there at night, among the rumble of traffic and the hum of factory machinery, one still sees coming out of the dark, like swarms of fireflies, pleasure boats full of Japanese leaning back on cushions as they are quietly punted along, listening and watching by the glow of paper lanterns to samisen music and geisha song.

But the picture of the night life of Tokyo would be criminally incomplete if one gave the impression that all was sex and frivolity. The capital is a city of everything; and in the midst of everything there is also the best: the best Western orchestras, the finest musicians, opera companies, ballet troupes, plays, revues, musical shows and variety artists are there for the thousands who long for them. Tokyo's intellectuals, the world of *interi* as they call themselves, are the most alert and eclectic in existence. Their passion for being up to date knows no end. They seem to pick up the *dernier cri* in Paris, London, New York, or Berlin, when it is still a tentative whisper. At the same time their own classical theatre, the Noh and Kabuki, where one sees some of the best acting in the world, their fine puppet art, Bunraku, their performances of *gagaku,* the ancient court music, and their symphonic arrangements for Japanese guitar, bamboo flutes and *koto,* a sort of harp evolved from ancient instruments, have undiminished vitality.

Noh performances in particular seemed to provoke greater reverence than ever, as if they were a kind of chain holding the Japanese to their original anchor in the storm of modern "becoming." Their ancient music, too, is like the wind of time bringing up from the other side of the world the first sounds of life setting out on its journey from chaos and old night.

Yet here I must leave the general impression of the capital. I am conscious that this is the merest of impressionist sketches of a fantastic complex. I could throw the Oxford Dictionary at it and still need more words, perhaps in Chinese, Sanskrit and Japanese, to catch all Tokyo's facts and tones. In the main I cling to the basic description of it used in the beginning as the "head of Japan." From Tokyo come the impulses of conscious administration, control, direction, invention, education, commerce, production and co-ordination of the teeming land. I have dealt with it at length, because what is true of it is true also of the other large cities of the land. Towns like Nagoya, Osaka, Kobe, Hiroshima, Fukuoka and Nagasaki, all have similar modern faces. Most of them have arisen as confidently and quietly from the ashes of the war. Since 1945 when it was a heap of rubble, Nagoya has performed the miracle of resurrection twice in a few years—in 1959 it was wrecked again by typhoon and flood. But Tokyo is the transformer, as it were, of the nation's energies: all other cities, except Kyoto, are subordinate to it.

During those first days in the new capital, when I was not bewildered, I was conscious of deep misgiving. My life has forced me again and again over the years to walk a wide beat from Africa to the Far East, from the Far East to Europe, from Europe to America and Africa. In the process I have been alarmed by the tendency of the human being to form a mass impression of a foreign country and then to fit its individuals into a collective abstract which is at best wildly approximate and as a rule wholly unreal. The modern cartoonist is the clearest example, and also the most dangerously adept, at this game of collective abstraction. The more I thought of this, the more I was convinced that the mass picture before my eyes would be hopelessly misleading unless I could find the individual within it. I realised that living in my comfortable Westernised hotel I would never succeed in doing this. So I determined that when I left the capital I would travel as much as possible the Japanese way, live only in Japanese inns and seek out only Japanese friends.

The moment I announced this intention, my Japanese friends rallied round me with enthusiasm, and I was in danger of being so firmly in the grip of their

Page 61 Neighbourhood children spy the photographer in a Tokyo suburb; 62 Ceremonies at a sumo tournament in Tokyo; 63 Slightly untraditional scene in the Nichigeki Music Hall; 64 Final scenes from a psychedelic play, *The Thousand and One Nights of Shinjuku,* written and presented by the poet Terayama; 65 The Kawasaki Steel Mill on the outskirts of Tokyo; 66 A woman sells masks at a stand in Asaksa, the Coney Island of Tokyo; 67 Hostess awaits customers in the doorway of a Shinjuku coffee shop; 68–69 Saturday night at the Tokyo à Go-Go; 70 Shigeo Nagashima, third baseman of the Yomiuri Giants, Japan's premier baseball star. He is the third-highest paid player in the world; 71 Two of the "Spiders," a Beatle-like rock group. This style of music, called Group-Sound, is sweeping Japan; 72 A father, taking his son to school, pauses before a shrine.

helpfulness as to be almost helpless myself! It was the great season of sightseeing and travel in Japan. Therefore, a friend insisted on taking me to the director of the extraordinarily efficient Japanese Tourist Bureau. He summoned his friends from railway, bus, inn and air organisations, and they arranged to take me from place to place in the Japanese way.

In a charming Japanese restaurant over dishes of tempura, prawns fried in vegetable oils and rice, all cooked by a master of the art, my friends gathered to speed me on my way. Some I had scarcely seen on this trip. They had come from far away, at great trouble and expense, though we had not met in all these years. As I slipped off my shoes at the entrance of the restaurant and was led by the Jochu-saw, the honourable Miss Waitress, dressed in a kimono, to a quiet room wide open to a garden and saw my old friends who had been waiting, relaxed on their *zabutons,* rising to greet me, I felt the collective unreality falling from me like a veil.

In every Japanese room and house there is an alcove, with a raised ledge inside it, called a *tokonoma.* In it the only ornament in the room, a hanging scroll, or *kakemono,* is displayed. It is not always the same and is changed according to the season, the day, or some special association in the mind of the owner. On this day the picture was of a flash of falling water and the shadow of a fish within bravely leaping the cataract. Below it was a dark-green vase with a single branch of twisted pine looking like an ancient dwarf tree itself. Then I understood. It was one of the great feast days of the year: boys' day. All the houses outside flew brightly coloured paper streamers shaped like carp from tall bamboo poles. The carp was a symbol of tenacity, endurance and longevity, just as the pine was, and it was flown like a flag over a boy's home as an image of what life and the nation expected of him. The place with its back to the *tokonoma* is always the seat of honour and my friends were determined to make me take it. After that we were long over our meal because each one of my Japanese friends had much to tell me.

The next day, a Sunday, I went with a very old friend to his home. He told me that recently his house had been burnt down, but nevertheless he insisted on taking me back with him. Spring and the tender evidence of reawakening was everywhere. The streets were full of boys in *yukata,* their kimono-like underwear, carrying palanquins to their shrines in long processions, twisting and turning with the burdens as the spirit—or, as they themselves would say, the *kaze* of *kami,* the breath from above—moved them, rather like a serpent coiling, uncoiling and recoiling. Although my friend was a director of a company, he had no private motorcar. Few Japanese can afford motorcars. Each day he travelled for two hours by train, bus and train to his work, and the same way back home again for two hours in the evening. At the end of the journey we were in a world of wooden houses, country lanes and gardens.

One saw at once that the roads were strange to motor traffic because they were full of potholes and puddles. And then suddenly at the side of a narrow lane we came to a garden with the black burnt-out shell of a home and in the midst of the cold cinders a single room of wood, paper and straw mats. The room was spotless and so bright that it shone like amber among the ashes. My friend's wife in kimono and two daughters in Western dress were there to greet us. Presently two of his sons, undergraduates at Tokyo University, came back from a baseball game, bats in hand. No one was the least put out at entertaining a foreigner in such circumstances, and before long I was being entertained like a prince in a palace and not in the one remaining room of a burnt-out house. Soon we sat down to a fourteen-course meal beautifully cooked by my hostess and daughters in a corner of the room. Conversation, at which the Japanese excel, bubbled up spontaneously from everyone.

When we could eat no more, we sang some ancient songs and finally my friend said: "Post-san, we would like to sing something for you."

I sat back, expecting some local ballad. When the song came I was too surprised for a second or two to believe my ears. Then I could doubt no longer. This pagan household had specially learnt, and were singing on my behalf, "Nearer, My God, to Thee"!

"As it was your Sunday," my host explained afterwards, "we thought you might like a hymn of your own religion."

As we sat there, a full moon rose over the trees and clumps of bamboo. Somehow in Japan the moon seems twice as big and impressive as in any other country. Or perhaps its natural effect is magnified by the response of the Japanese to its presence. If ever there has been a nation whose spirit is swung by the moon—like the tides of the sea—it is the Japanese nation. But this has negative aspects. For instance, one of the most brutal Japanese commanders in my prison camp was cruel only when the moon was full. Before then, as a rule, he was a gentle and amiable person, but as the moon waxed, so he would change until, in the moment of its fullness, he was struck with sadistic madness. Then he was capable of terrible atrocities. Yet once they were committed he became gentle again, like one purified through shedding innocent blood.

But in their positive responses it is the moon and not the sun that contains the imagination of the Japanese. So as we sat there together at this gathering of friends, my host, hostess and children began to compare and recite verses in its honour. My host, his eyes on the light falling through the bamboos on the ashes of his house, quoted from an ancient poem: "All grief can be annihilated by just gazing at the moon." He quoted also a Buddhist monk from long ago who commanded his followers "to keep the mind-heart in harmony like the full moon." Then they asked me, too, for a poem about the moon. All I could remember seemed too romantic and out of place. So, my eyes on the burnt-out shell of their home, I told them the story related to me by the African Bushman, of how the moon, seeing men afraid of death, sent them a message saying: "As I dying am renewed again, so will you in dying be renewed again."

The family drew their breath in sharply with appreciation when I had finished and the head of the house said, "How strange and wonderful. When the Lord Buddha was dying and he saw all the animals gathered round him weeping bitterly, he pointed at the moon and said: 'As the moon dies and dying is renewed again, so shall I be renewed through death,' and all the animals believed him and were comforted."

"All except the serpent," the youngest son exclaimed. "That is why everyone hates serpents to this day."

IV

---∞---

On the Tokaido Road

From Tokyo I set out for Kyoto by the Tokaido. For thousands of years the Tokaido, the eastern highway beside the sea, was the great road of history in Japan. Along it the Yamato peoples of the south-west pushed northeastwards in their wars against the aborigines, the hairy Ainu, the Emishi or barbarians, as the Yamatos called them. The Emishi fell back slowly, fighting fiercely, and the wars lasted for centuries. For long the Tokaido was the road along which samurai legions marched and counter-marched. But once the shoguns, the great overlords of Japan, took the power of government from the Emperor and established themselves in Yedo (now Tokyo), the Tokaido lost its austerity and became one of the most colourful, magnificent, romantic, vital and eventful highways of all time.

The Emperor and his court were confined in the old capital, Kyoto, where they led lives of an intricate, elegant and polite fiction, writing poems, compos-ing music, organising moon-gazing parties, having complicated love affairs, studying the art of arranging flowers and sipping sea-green tea. The real power, the will and the purpose were in Yedo. Hence all year long between the two cities, along the Tokaido, passed soldiers, vagabonds, pilgrims, minstrels, priests, nuns, storytellers, merchants, spies, wrestlers, imperial emissaries, companies of actors, painters, daimyos—the feudal barons of Japan with their knights and squires—all to pay homage to emperor and overlord. Sometimes, too, there appeared a foreign face in the colourful throng, a Jesuit priest, perhaps a prisoner of some provincial authority because, despite the decree banning all foreigners, he had landed secretly in the far south to carry on the missionary work started with such zeal by St. Francis Xavier in 1549. Or a party of stout Dutch merchants, who were allowed a single trading post at Nagasaki on condition that once a year they came to turn somersaults in the streets of Tokyo, thus publicly degrading themselves and winding up this humiliating action by spitting on the Cross in the presence of the shogun and his court.

At the end of each diurnal lap of the road, inns, shops, brothels, teahouses, shrines and temples sprang up, and late at night and early in the morning the hospices rang and vibrated with the arrival and departure, the song, dance, talk, quarrels, clatter and fisticuffs of this variegated throng. Fortunately the splendour, the arrogance, elegance, exaggeration, variety, as well as the vulgar, coarse, yet ever vital rhythm of the flood of life along this highway are preserved forever in Hiroshige's famous prints and in the *Hiza Kurige,* a great Rabelaisian piece of literature written under the name of Jippensha Ikku. The *Hiza Kurige* is as important for an understanding of the inborn dominants of Japanese character as are the sophisticated refinements of the *Tale of Genji* of Lady Murasaki, the *Pillow Book* of her hated rival, Sei Shonagon, or the poetry of Bashō.

Unfortunately, I was forced to do most of the journey by train, yet that, too, had compensations. In Japan the roads are bad and motorcars too expensive for most Japanese, but part of the reason for the efficiency and comfort of the trains is, I believe, the mystique that the Japanese retain about trains and locomotives. That was started on the highest level for them by the Emperor Meiji. The first train ever seen by the Japanese was brought to Japan from America by Commodore Perry in 1854. But the first railway was built between Tokyo and Yokohama by British engineers. When the Emperor opened it in 1872, he treated it as a religious occasion, appearing with his retinue in the most ancient of court robes, and before boarding the first train, he commended the train to his subjects as the new way to prosperity and happiness. Certainly of all the officials in Japan today, the stationmaster, inviolate in his purple uniform and red-and-gold cap, still walks his platform, like an admiral pacing his quarter-deck, aware that he represents his emperor. He has, too, many practical reasons for satisfaction. His trains are always full. It is the favourite Japanese means of travelling. Travelling by train brings out all that is gay and carefree in the people and particularly in the third class, where the coaches look as if all the passengers, talking, laughing, exchanging information and often sharing their food, belonged to one family.

In Japanese trains I found one thing that I had never seen before: a vase of fresh flowers suspended in a bracket over the lavatory seats and over the washstands.

Unfortunately, I left Tokyo in heavy rain. The landscape was invisible and only here and there, close to the railway, could I make out the ghost of a concrete apartment-settlement around some factory or mill that might have been a suburb of Paris or Rome. So I turned my attention to my fellow passengers. Immediately I was struck by the fact that there are three kinds of Japanese faces: one, perhaps the oldest, is a Polynesian-Sumatran face; the second, South Chinese; and the third, heart-shaped, with high forehead, arched nose, the bridge thinner and higher in a modified Roman manner, mouth smaller, eyes well-shaped, large and slanted, and the hair thicker than that of the other two.

What sort of people produced these distinctive types and where did they originate? It is customary to think of the third as having come out of Asia through Korea to Japan before recorded history, of the second as being of South Chinese origin, and of the first as mysterious and unaccountable. Going only by the evidence of my eyes, I have a hunch that this strain came from the ocean towards the deep southwest of Japan. If this is so, the people came to the Land of the Rising Sun so long ago that no trace of their migration is to be found even in the myths and legends of Japan. Yet in the language that the Japanese speak even today there is a vocabulary that cannot be related to China, Korea, or Margoba and that has a marked Polynesian-Malay affinity. There is also the fact that the deepest strata of the Japanese mind are in its

Shinto level, where the Japanese instinctively abandons himself to a profound nature worship of the kind I have found among the aborigines of Java, the Badoeis in the heart of the Sunda country.

Significant in this regard is the fact that the most sacred of all the Japanese shrines is the one at Ise. There the mirror, which is the symbol of the Emperor's divine authority, is kept, and there before the war he went to report on his accession and on all the other high acts of state to his ancestor, the Sun Goddess. The simple building of wooden pillars, timbered walls and thatched roof is like the traditional buildings I have seen in parts of Indonesia. Moreover, Ise, it is generally accepted, is the purest survival of the pattern of Japanese architecture before the invasion of Chinese culture in the sixth and seventh centuries, and for this reason Ise is pulled down and rebuilt every twenty years, strictly in accordance with an immutable design handed down from the unrecorded past. To date, there have been forty-nine proved rebuildings of the shrine. At the moment shrines are out of fashion in Japan. The psychological chauvinistic use the military made of the Shinto cult to prepare Japan for the war has made them suspect. The first time I was in Japan my friends saw to it that I visited their most famous shrines before anything else. Now they urged me to visit temples, gardens, factories, the countryside, and suggested no shrines, except Ise. Here is an illustration of the sort of emotions that Ise evokes: a Japanese Cabinet Minister was assassinated there by an ordinary spectator simply because he was seen to lift with the tip of his walking stick the simple silk curtain which hangs between the public and the inmost shrine and through which only the Emperor was normally allowed to pass. Not the Cabinet Minister but the assassin had a public memorial raised to him! Surely this sort of action is only possible because the image of this building has been present in the spirit of the Japanese from the beginning of their history. Yet no kind of building could be less suitable for the Japanese climate. Like the Japanese house, it is not really designed for the cold Arctic winds of their winter. Anyone who is tempted, therefore, to explain the evolution of civilisation in terms of environmental challenges and responses would do well to reflect on the astonishing phenomenon of Ise, as well as on the frail wood and paper houses of the humble citizen. They might be surprised at the vitality and tenacity of the primordial sense of their origin that human beings carry within their blood and also at its influence on their values.

But to return to the three types of Japanese. Of course, there are many variations. Like all races, the Japanese by now are exceedingly mixed, even with the aborigines, the Ainu, the Emishi, whom they conquered and practically eliminated. Yet the fact that these types still do exist testifies to the antiquity of the three strains. Beside me in the train sat a Japanese with a refined face of the type favoured by actors and painters. Across the aisle was a party of middle-aged tourists. We began talking, and the man beside me told me that he was a medical student in his fifth year. For years now he had made extra money for his studies by conducting tourists round Japan, and the party opposite was his. He had prepared himself with imagination and thoroughness for his task, but by the time we met he was inclined to be despondent about his charges.

He had three volumes of lovely copies of the coloured woodcuts of the two great masters of the Japanese landscape: Hokusai and Hiroshige. The illustrations were all relevant to the journey along the Tokaido and seemed to me to cover almost the whole of human reactions to life and nature: Hokusai, in love with the elegant line and the quick impression and at the same time provoked to a savage humour by the excesses and pretensions of his time as, for instance, when an aristocratic procession is transformed by his brush into a train of grass-hoppers bearing a mantis in a litter; Hiroshige, elegiac, gentler, more accepting and charged to the full with the mystery of all things from the pebbles at a ford to the clouds menacing Fuji itself with blue slanted rain. Yet, the young Japanese told me, he had tried in vain to interest his charges in the illustrations. Worse, at Ise they had even refused to get out of their cars to walk towards the several shrines there. It was astonishing, he declared, how often this happened, and he shook his head sadly as we said good-bye, remarking that he often wondered why people travelled at all.

I left him in the train to do by road the section of the journey through the

Fuji National Park. But it was still raining heavily and visibility was hardly a hundred yards. So I made straight for my first Japanese inn among the foothills of Fuji itself. At the entrance to the inn I took off my wet shoes, put on a pair of light slippers and signed my name in a register at the request of the only man I was to see in the inn for the duration of my stay. The traveller who journeys in the Japanese way finds himself handed over entirely to the care of women at his places of rest. Somewhere in the background, no doubt, there is a male director, even a company of men drawing annual dividends, but responsibility for the traveller's comfort, food, rest and amusement rests entirely on large staffs of women. To me their grace and efficiency in looking after the traveller were an endless source of amazement. A charming "Miss Waitress" was immediately allotted to me and she conducted me along a wooden corridor, unstained but polished so that it shone like a mirror. Through the paper walls of the rooms we passed came the soft light of the grey day. The stillness and peace within were broken only by the remote patter and swish of the rain without. At the entrance to my room, Miss Waitress pushed the *shoji,* or wooden doors, apart. Beyond was a small square hall with a sunken floor, of tiles made out of river stones. Behind more *shoji* were a lavatory, the bathroom and my room. I was enchanted to see that my room had no number, but written over it in Chinese characters was the name: Evening Primrose. Behind the *shoji,* raised some inches above the tiles, were the pale-gold *tatami* of my room. Even my slippers were too hard and coarse for the *tatami,* so I left them outside and entered the room in my socks.

The room was without decoration or adornment except that in the *tokonoma* was a dark-blue vase with a long neck and a single sprig of azalea in it. In the centre was only a low black-lacquer table barely nine inches high. For the rest the beauty of the room came from its proportions, the grain of the wood in the uprights, the quality of the paper in walls and doors, the way the paper continually absorbed the light all around one, and finally from the clean fit and perfect weave of the straw in the *tatami.*

A European room forces itself upon your attention, the furniture and pictures in it try continually to impress you, if not to possess you. The Japanese room tries to leave you free or, at most, to serve you. Out of a paper cupboard in the wall was brought some *zabuton* for me to squat on beside the shining black table. Then the *shoji* to the outside world were opened wide and Miss Waitress left me with a profound obeisance and a request to be excused for a minute.

All the best rooms in Japanese inns are on the ground floor at the back of the building, facing the garden. In the Japanese architect's vision of his art, house and garden are one. Indeed, it is difficult to decide which of the two constitutes the better half. Only one thing is certain. If the architect has been true to his art, the room meets the garden almost at ground level, so that while you squat on your *zabuton* the garden appears framed in the wooden supports of the building like the precious landscape painting of an old master. The room, unadorned and made out of natural and organic materials, will have an immediate affinity with the garden, not separating you from it but making you feel as if you are in some sheltered extension of it, sharing in its processes of growth.

Now the garden at the sill of my room, with the fume and mist of the heavy rain giving it a depth of space it did not really possess, was designed to represent a great landscape in miniature. In the centre, level with my eyes as I sat, was a little stream flowing between ancient pines to drop some ten feet into a miniature lake. It emerged again to twist and turn, like a great river on its way to the sea, through the grass and between diminutive hills of the garden, to vanish finally behind a small bamboo grove. Where the stream emerged from the tiny lake was a bridge arched over it, and at the top of the arch it broke into a sort of curved zigzag after the fashion of many a temple-garden bridge. I remembered a priest explaining the zigzag arch to me: "Evil is like a rhinoceros. It always charges in straight lines. We break the line of the bridge so that evil cannot cross, but falls over the edge to drown in the deep water in the middle."

Presently Miss Waitress reappeared with some hot green tea. She sank on her knees beside the little table and served me with the delicate, refreshing liquid. While I was sipping the tea, she opened another paper cupboard to produce a *yukata,* a light cotton under-kimono, and a sober quilted kimono of black with a pinpoint gold stripe. She then said, *"O-furo dekita yo* [The honourable bath is ready]*."*

Turning my face to the wall, as etiquette demanded, I slipped off my clothes and held out my arms for her to put the clean cotton kimono over my shoulders. I followed her across the tiled square to the bathroom. She ushered me into the room and, bowing low again, left me to my bath.

A great deal has been written about the role of bathing in the life of the Japanese because it is one of the main events in their daily round. There is no one in the land from coolie to emperor who does not bathe at least once a day. He does so either in the privacy of his own home, in the company of others at the hotel bathroom, or at one of the many public baths in the big cities, where nowadays you can bathe in any way ever invented from Turkish, Finnish and sulphur baths to Roman tubs filled with milk or water which has been pumped full of vitamins and hormones. Indeed, when I was first in Japan, there were still villages where, in the summer evenings, the people put their wooden tubs outside their houses next to those of their friends, lit fires underneath them, got inside the tubs and while the water warmed up exchanged the gossip of the day and settled the foreign affairs of the nation. But whichever way it is done, the bath means more to the Japanese than to us: it is not merely an act of physical hygiene but a ritual designed to cleanse the mind and spirit of contamination from the imperfections and unreality of the physical world. This need for a ritual of purification in the Japanese spirit goes very deep. Bathing is not the only form. Suicide, death, traditional sport, all are preceded by their own prescribed forms of purification. Thus even the wrestler, before he tackles his opponent in the ring, will repeatedly scatter coarse salt on the floor around him—salt, too, purifies. But of all forms, the bath appears the oldest and most universal, perhaps because right at the beginning of time the brother of the Sun Goddess herself, after his vain attempt to bring back his dead wife from the underworld, was only allowed to return to life after taking a bath of purification in the stream dividing it from the world of death.

Nothing illustrates the different attitude to the bath more, perhaps, than the fact that the Japanese never combine lavatory and bathroom in one. Today in Western-style hotels in Japan it may be different. But in the Japanese inn and in the house they are separate and even have separate pairs of slippers outside their *shoji*, carefully marked for use in one and not in the other. Also the bathroom is not an airless compartment tucked into the wasteland of the establishment. It has the place of honour with a full view of the garden. Since a whole Japanese family will use the same bath water, starting with the head of the house and ending with the servants, no washing of the body is done in the bath itself. Wooden tubs of hot water are provided for that and all the washing is done outside before one enters the bath. You get into the bath for the warmth, the feel of the water and the effect on your spirit. You do not lie in it. The Japanese bath is made to be sat in, with the water up to your neck as if it were some kind of easy chair. It is extraordinary how, sitting in it, you feel released from the gravity of the earth and the dead weight of your own matter. Suddenly you are free in your mind to enjoy without impediment the garden, and to follow the thoughts evoked by it. After the noise and the fever of Tokyo, I shall not easily forget my baths in the stillness of Evening Primrose.

Back in the room, my own clothes had vanished and, I am tempted to say, with them my European personality. In my years in prison camp I had often reflected on the matter, so I was not surprised by the realisation of how much we in the West rely on externals, on possessions and on material things to sustain our assumptions of superiority. But how well, how lightly and how far you can travel with little in Japan! One suit, a set of underclothing, a shirt, a pair of socks, a tie, a razor and a handkerchief or two are all you need. At every inn your suit is taken away, sponged and pressed; your underclothes, shirt, socks and handkerchief are washed; and the inn meanwhile provides all you need. Instead of pyjamas you have a clean *yukata;* instead of a suit, a kimono. You do not need even a comb or a toothbrush because in your room there are a new toothbrush, toothpaste and comb, all sealed in paper, awaiting you. Putting on my kimono, I relaxed on my *zabuton,* and since it was still raining, I read for some hours.

Page 89 The mountain glimpsed from far across the Izu Peninsula on a bright spring morning; 90 Fuji reflected in a stubbled rice field; 91 Women farm workers labour under a cloud-wrapped Fuji in the Five Lakes area; 92 A railroad worker makes his way home in the Oiso area; 93 A pair of motorcyclists roar over a road in the Hakone National Park; 94–95 Pilgrims on the top of Mount Sichimen worship in the sunrise before the enduring shape of Fuji; 96 These monks spend their lives at a monastery on a mountain facing Fuji; 97 Fuji framed in a gate of the Sichimen monastery; 98 The mountain seen through the pilot's window during the regular Tokyo–Osaka flight; 99 The mountain seen from directly overhead; 100–101 Peasants work their fields overwhelmed by the mountain near the classic Tokaido Road; 102 Blue Fuji, at the instant of the moonrise; 103 On the evening of the full moon it seems to leap from the crater; 104 The bare branches form an Oriental tracery against the face of the mountain.

I had with me an anthology of Japanese poetry, the poems written first in Chinese characters, then in Roman letters and finally in English. Like the garden, as if to support the familiar Western criticism of Japanese art, the poems were miniature. Some ran to fifty or seventy lines. But most were minute pieces of five lines, each of no more than thirty-one syllables. Even these were considered verbose, and in the end Japanese poetry reached its greatest heights in the development of *haiku,* a chip, a flake of a poem of only three lines of seventeen syllables.

Again it is astonishing how old, consistent and deep is this impulse of the Japanese to find the great in the small, to separate the superfluous from the essential. What was interesting, too, was how much more impressive these little poems were in Chinese writing. I know only a few hundred of the simplest Chinese characters and one must know close on two thousand to read even the most simple items in a newspaper. Some six thousand are in ordinary use. Scholars draw on fifteen thousand and more, depending on the depth of their learning. But since Chinese writing, adopted by the Japanese centuries ago, is a kind of picture writing and therefore at an archaic level of the collective spirit of mankind, it tends to be universal. My little knowledge was just enough to see how the shape of the characters and the thought expressed in the little poems added to the meaning of one another. Thus the character of a man reclining by a tree represents repose, at ease; or a heart at an open window, anxiety. Written with a brush and not a fountain pen, they are extremely beautiful.

Of course a great many practical objections can be raised against this method of writing. Both the Chinese and the Japanese are acutely aware of them all and have anxiously searched their hearts and minds this past century as to whether they should change over to our system. Communist China indeed, with its dialectical materialism, is now said to be on the verge of changing, and if it does Japan will have to follow. Science and industry no doubt will rejoice at the change. But the artist, the poet and the priest, in fact all who serve the first images of meaning in life, will feel the poorer.

I was still reading when Miss Waitress reappeared to see whether I needed refreshment. She apologised, as if she were to blame, for the rain and the weather, saying that otherwise I would have had such a perfect view of the great mountain, which she called with a loving note of reverence, "*Fuji-san* [Lord Fuji]." Oddly enough, I had just read a *haiku* by Bashō, the great poet and supreme master of this minute and endearing form of art. He had come here some three hundred years before, when the journey was not easy or cheap, just to see the mountain. Then, too, it had rained, yet despite his disappointment he had written in a room, I imagine, very like Evening Primrose the *haiku*:

Kiri—shigure	Though Fuji is hidden
Fuji wo minu hi zo	In the mist and rain of winter,
Omoshiroki	On such a day, too,
	There is a joy.

I showed her the *haiku* and remarked that it expressed my own feelings. Instantly there was a change in her attitude to me. She had been the Miss Waitress, courteous and efficient, but now suddenly I seemed to her an individual. She smiled and said she knew the *haiku* well. Like Basho, she hoped, I would have better luck in the morning, for did I realise that the weather had improved for him since he also was able to write the *haiku,* which I later found in my anthology:

Kumo kiri no	As I stand deep in thought on
Shibashi Bankei o	the lake shore,
Tsukushi keri	Fuji in the changing mist
	Presents me with all its hundred
	views.

I am certain she could not have been more startled over my interest in Japanese poetry than I was at the display of such apt and ready knowledge in a person of so humble a position and upbringing. I could not imagine a housemaid or waitress in Britain or in America quoting Shelley or Byron or Whitman. From then on I was to be amazed continually by the keen and living appreciation of their culture among the humblest of Japanese. If ever I was puzzled by a wayside shrine, by a piece of poetry, or wanted the information about some legend, work of art, or temple for which a locality was renowned, I would find the Miss Waitresses in inns, Miss Conductresses in the buses, the Mr. Gardeners, Mr. Taxi-drivers, and Mr. Coolies, unfailing sources of enlightenment. It was most rewarding how instantly an interest in these things brought forth a warm, generous response and a touching solicitude for my enlightenment.

Not knowing this at the time, I could not help showing some surprise, and Miss Waitress, so shy as to be almost inaudible, asked whether I had not known that Japanese women, too, were great poets. Some of the finest poetry of Japan had been written by women from as far back as the eighth century. To this day many Japanese women wrote poetry. No, she did not herself, but she loved it, and *haiku* was her favourite form.

I asked her please to recite the *haiku* she liked best. She said it was very difficult, there were so many, but perhaps it was:

Rakkwa eda ni	I thought I saw the fallen flower
Kaeru to mireba	Returning to its branch
Kocho kana	Only to find it was a butterfly.

The *haiku* was not in my anthology and we had great difficulty in arriving at a meaning for me. Apart from the fact that my knowledge of the language is fragmentary, the language itself has no easy parallels in European or any other form of speech. The nearest known group of languages to which it roughly corresponds is the so-called Ural-Altaic, but the parallel is so technical and dim as to be misleading. Even its great neighbour the Chinese language is of a totally different character, and though Japan has freely borrowed from it and greatly enriched itself in the process, rather as English did by drawing on

Latin and Greek, the language remains very much a structure of its own. Superficially it looks easy enough. Pronouncing it is far easier than Chinese. Moreover it has no number, article, or gender, but the moment one starts to speak it difficulties in their hundreds arise. There is not merely the inexhaustible vocabulary but the fact that organically it is differently conceived from any of our Western tongues. Even the fundamental division of infinite, present, past and future does not exist for it in the same degree as for us. It seems to be organised on the basis of potential states of being, possibility and moods, and the verbs are used to describe things that have not yet happened, might happen, probably will happen, are about to happen, are happening, or have definitely happened. Not time but the element of probability and the relation of the speaker to the one spoken to seem to dominate the structure of the language. As a result it is a tongue full of allusion, suggestion, mood and association of endless poetic nuance and possibility, which is the despair of the abstract thinkers and the logical positivists of our world. It is significant that the more scientific and technological Japan has become the more it has drawn on Chinese, which is a precise and rational tongue, for the appropriate terms, just as the English in a similar predicament draw on Latin and Greek. Finally, to complicate the complex, Japanese women tend to have a vocabulary of their own. They seem to be the chatelaines of the first speech of the Japanese as the priests at Ise are of their first forms of building. In their speech and above all their poetry the Yamato words abound. It is not surprising, therefore, that we did not arrive at the version I have given here of the favourite *haiku* of Miss Waitress until we had been joined in the evening by a student, a friend of Japanese friends, who was coming with me to Kyoto.

I went to meet the young student at the hotel of the mountain resort. Since my own clothes had vanished I went out in kimono and wooden sandals. At the entrance to the inn I was given an immense umbrella made of oiled paper, painted over with Chinese characters and exactly like those seen in Hiroshige's "Fifty-three stages of the Tokaido." It kept the rain off me admirably, and as I strutted along I saw the country people, smocks and *yukata* tucked up to their loins, going about their business under similar protection. It was indeed a complete Hiroshige scene with Hiroshige people and slanted blue Hiroshige rain. Outside even more than within I was impressed how Boshō's first *haiku* about Fuji was not an aesthetic pretension. Though it was invisible in the rain, I was strangely aware of the mountain's presence. It was as if the arrangement of the earth, the shape of the houses, the line of the streets and the contours all conformed to a definite pattern determined by the pull of an invisible magnet.

However tired one becomes of the conventional picture of Fuji seen in pictures, lacquer, metal, glass, porcelain, fabrics and literature, there is no denying that it is one of the greatest mountains of the earth. This is not due to its size—it is not much more than twelve thousand feet high—but to its shape and position in the storm-tossed earth of Japan. It is the mountain of perfect proportion. I have loved mountains all my life and climbed some of the highest like Kilimanjaro, which is close on twenty thousand feet and not unlike a kind of African Fuji. The great ones all have their own personality and character and present in their own individual way a challenge to men. These mountains in their size and in their forbidding nature provoke a special type of human being to take up the challenge. In the process of overcoming them, he conquers something in himself, and the achievement, however undefined and irrational, is not to be underrated. But Fuji draws to itself more the pilgrim than the mountaineer because it is the mountain not of challenge but of resolution. The first time I saw it was at dawn from the railway line along the shore of Tokyo Bay, and at once it made the most wonderful music in my senses, rising like a vortex of purple sound out of the wine-red sea of dawn to achieve a white cone of elegance and perfection in the blue sky. It expressed the thing about true mountains which makes them sacred in the natural symbolism of the human spirit.

I was not surprised, therefore, that it had remained sacred to the Japanese and that thousands of pilgrims still climb it every year, nor that Hokusai painted a hundred different views of Fuji, and Hiroshige close on fifty. Nor did I wonder at the look of fulfilment that I had seen on the face of an old photographer I had met in Tokyo who had spent fifty-four years of his life taking photographs of Fuji. What adds to the sense of the miraculous inspired by Fuji is the feeling that its beauty and resolution have not been achieved without passion and agony. It is still a fire mountain. It is true it erupted last at the beginning of the eighteenth century, but it still gives one the feeling that the ancient fires burn on in its heart, ready to flare up again if forced, for a distribution of folds and ruffles in the earth's crust around Fuji continues ceaselessly and makes that district the most earthquake-shaken in the whole of Japan. The Japanese have many names and adjectives to describe this most evocative of mountains, from "Lord Fuji" and "August Mountain" to "Rich Scholar" and "the deathless one," but my favourite is the simple and typical Japanese understatement: "that which is without equal."

When I returned at last with the young student to my room, Miss Waitress excused herself to fetch our evening meal: Asa-gohan, or evening rice. It came soon on two trays of unstained wood, polished so that the grain stood out like the lines on the tip of the human thumb. Its beauty again was entirely in the nature of the wood, its proportions, and the craftsmanship of the maker. There was no external decoration. Our food, too, was beautifully laid out. The Japanese cook, far more than the Chinese chef who is considered to be his superior, is concerned as much with the appearance as the taste of his food. My tray looked like a still life by an old master: hors d'oeuvre, consisting of a square of cold savoury rice, contained in a transparent wall of dark-green seaweed; a slice of brown bean-cake; some white leeks and vivid green gherkins; a scroll of black seaweed with some crimson fish and bean-paste on a crimson lacquer dish, shaped and glowing like a maple leaf in the autumn. Next to it was a lacquer bowl of an ancient bronze colour covered with a lid, containing some hot fish soup. Beside these was a small round porcelain bowl of blue and white containing a black sauce, and a flat dark-blue dish with neat slices of pink and white raw fish on it. Resting on a little porcelain trestle, a pair of wooden chopsticks (still joined at one end to show that they had not been used) were laid out on the side nearest me. We broke our chopsticks and began to eat. The fresh wood of the chopsticks added a flavour rather like that of wood smoke to the food. Halfway through the meal a crayfish, cracked open and with the flesh sliced into pieces for easy eating, was produced on another delicate porcelain platter. The meal ended with a bowl of rice and green tea. The rice was delicious. I think Japanese rice is the best in the world. It is so good that very little of it is eaten in Japan; most of it is exported abroad, where the money thus earned is used to buy cheaper rice for consumption in Japan.

All the while Miss Waitress sat on her knees by our side, seeing that we were never without food or tea and entertaining us with the most varied and intelligent conversation. When the meal was done and cleared away she and my student friend entertained me until late by singing songs of the district and helping me to translate the words and discover the legends and history behind the music. And since it was getting cold at that altitude at night, I asked if I could have another hot bath, and apologised for making the request so late. Miss Waitress smiled and said it was most usual. She herself had already had five baths that day. "Whenever I have a free moment," she told me, "I have a bath. It relaxes and refreshes me."

"But how do you manage to have so much hot water always ready?" I asked.

"Oh, Lord Fuji does it all." She laughed and explained that it came in bamboo pipes straight from one of the many volcanic hot springs in the area.

When I came out of my bath, I found not only the *shoji* shut against the night but also the wooden outside screen and the *amado* drawn together. The table had gone. In its place were the *futon,* the sleeping quilts, piled three deep. A reading lamp, glowing warmly in a paper shade, was standing behind the silk pillows. I crept in between silk covers and had the best night's rest I had had in years. Whenever I woke there was the lovely sound of the rain and I thought this is how a house should be: a shelter and yet not a separation from nature. Every now and then some Hiroshige character went by on his wooden sandals, his *geta* making that lovely sound the Japanese call "Kara-koro, kara-koro, kara-koro." When I first slept in a Japanese inn thirty-four years before, the sound was so urgent in the streets outside that it had the same exciting effect on my imagination as a troop of cavalry going by in the darkness of night.

Alas! I did not have the poet's luck. The next day it was raining harder than ever. Though we travelled far by road, through the pass called the "Gate of Kwanto," by the "three islands," through the "valley of the greater boiling," over the "long tail" and "the maiden's passes," on by the "valley of lesser boiling" and over "the pass of the ten provinces," we saw no sign of Fuji or any of the five lakes in which it is mirrored on a clear day so perfectly that the reflection can hardly be told from the reflected. It rained thus all the way to Kyoto.

V

Kyoto

At a glance from the railway station, Kyoto did nothing to justify my definition of it as the heart of Japan. Even the rain could not conceal the fact that this ancient city of one and a quarter million inhabitants had suffered a severe measure of impetuous, perfunctory and somewhat careless and slovenly modernisation. The square in front of me, filled with reeling trams, reckless motor traffic and crowds of preoccupied people in European clothes, suggested little more than a provincial variant of the bewildering Tokyo theme.

But when I paused to look deeper I soon realised that there was a difference. First there were the human beings behind the European clothes. They were taller and straighter than in Tokyo, and my student companion drew my attention to the clear complexion, serene expression and proud bearing of the women: they are the most beautiful in Japan. But more important, men and women had little of the restless, seeking hunger I had felt among the Tokyo crowds. They looked more centred and content. But why?

A gust of wind tore the slanted rain apart and there, as if in answer, rose the curved roof of the great Higashi Hogan-ji, the temple of the Jodo Shinshu sect whose faith is epitomised in the command: "*Nama Amida Batsu:* let us worship the Buddha Amida, source of infinite light."

It is not my favourite temple, but that one glimpse of it was enough to remind me that in Kyoto I was about to walk again in the presence of all that is vital and living in the history of the spirit in Japan. Kyoto is the city most concerned with Japan's search for a release from the terrible contradictions in the national character. Tokyo is obsessed with immediacy; it is the capital of the world without; Kyoto is the capital of the world within. When the Emperor is enthroned, the solemn ceremony is enacted not in Tokyo but in Kyoto. When it was first founded toward the end of the eighth century after profound new impulses had been released in the Japanese spirit by the first contacts with Korean and Chinese culture and the discovery of the "84,000 doctrines" of the Lord Buddha, it was called Heian-Kyo, or Capital of Peace. Alas! It did not remain that for long. The spirit, like the flesh, has its hubris. War with and among priests and monks, struggle for power between emperors and feudal barons, prolonged civil war launched by baron against baron as well as earthquake and fire wracked the city. But somehow, through it all, Kyoto stuck closely to the blueprint of faith which had first determined its being. Even the Imperial Court, when deprived of all worldly power (however one might be tempted to laugh today at its aesthetic pretensions, ceremonious absurdities and excesses of form), pursued for centuries with devotion and elegance the human heart's nostalgia for beauty that will reach beyond the grave. After all, it was this effete society of the Kyoto court that inspired Lady Murasaki's six volumes of the exquisite *Tale of Genji* and Sei Shonagon's profound and malicious *Pillow Book* and produced numerous artists and poets whose influence on an impressionable nation was of immense significance.

But the real and the positive glory of Kyoto was the patient, selfless and sustained work of saints, priests, monks and nuns. Either by faith or by collaborating with the temporal power, they raised the fifteen hundred temples, built the two hundred shrines, inspired the contemplative villas, the gold, silver, lacquered and the plain wood, thatch, paper and straw pavilions that stare untroubled at their own reflections in the clear waters of the thousand and one gardens, ponds and streams of the city. Many of these buildings are of an original and incomparable beauty. Their names alone are enough to evoke the exalted status of their founders and resound in the imagination like a roll call of the history of the spirit in Japan. For instance, to select only a few among the fifteen hundred, there is the Tofuku-ji or Temple of Eastern Happiness; the Saihō-ji or Temple of Western Fragrance; the Daitoku-ji or Temple of Great Virtue; Myoshin-ji or Temple of the Dedicated Heart; Sanzen-in or Temple of the Three Thousand; i.e., of the Universe; Ninna-ji or Temple of Benevolent Harmony; Ryoan-ji or Temple of the Dragon's Repose; Tenryu-ji or Temple of the Celestial Dragon; Nanzen-ji or Temple of Enlightenment; Daikaku-ji or Temple of Great Science; the Chion-ji or Temple of Gratitude; the Shiren-in or Temple of the Blue Lotus; the Kiyomizu-dera or Temple of Pure Fountains; the Daigo-ji or Temple of Absolute Illumination; the Myoho-in or Temple of Miraculous Law; the Sukan-ji or Temple of Serenity and Peace, and so on and on. No less evocative are the names of pavilions and villas like the Shugaku-in or Villa of the Doctrine; the Shisen-do or Poet's Pavilion; the Kinkaku-ji or Golden Pavilion; the Ginkaku-ji or Silver Pavilion; the Shishi-Den or Imperial Purple Pavilion; the Gepparo or Waves by Moonlight Pavilion; and Seiryō-Den or Pavilion of Sweet Coolness.

Unlike the Hongashi temples, few of these buildings are immediately on view. They are shy of the external world and of ostentation and display. They have to be sought out where they shelter in their own discreetly chosen ground, in the miniature valleys, glades, meadows and ample fold of the purple mountains. In this they are true to the instinctive mistrust the Japanese feel for the world of matter and appearances. Moreover, though many of these temples are vast treasure houses of works of great and delicate art, these treasures, too, are hidden. They are shown as a rule only to the devout on their own specific day.

As a result, no one knows precisely the grand sum of masterpieces preserved in temple and shrine. All I know myself is that when I have visited the right temple on the right day I have been rewarded with a glimpse of a scroll of writing or painting on silk as if it had just fallen glistening from the master's brush.

All this and more was brought forcibly to my mind in the few days I spent in the city. The rain abated, but the clouds hung low over the purple mountains and the mist smoked over quicksilver streams, tranquil lakes and burnished ponds. From the highest peak of the Mountain of Wisdom called Shimeigadake, or The Four Splendours, the city was invisible most of the time. When it did appear briefly it was as a blurred image of itself on the gleaming shores of the great Lake Biwa. It was all most disappointing because the views from Mt. Hiei are rich in historical, spiritual and poetical associations. Lake Biwa itself, with the vast primeval forest and clear-cut mountains hemming it in, has perhaps the favourite eight views of classical Japan: the autumn moon seen from Ishiyama; the evening snow on Mt. Hira; the sunset at Seta; the evening bell of Miidera; the boats sailing back from Yabase; the bright sky with a breeze at Awazu; the rain by night at Karasaki; and the wild geese alighting at Katata.

Of the eight views, only rain by night at Karasaki seemed visible there. In some ways I would not have had it otherwise, because mist, cloud and shadow brought out the profound, innate colour of the landscape as no bright sun could have done. Along the old temple paths azaleas and wisteria in full bloom burned like flames. All along the steep slopes flanking the roads in the mountain passes they illuminated the dense mist with ruby fire, and where the mist was thickest wisteria flashed out of the gloom like a frill of violet lace on a fringe of waterfall. The temples and shrines showed up in isolation and made the encounter a private meeting. Yet I was careful not to see too many temples. I took to heart the ancient Japanese exhortation that the many in life can be mastered only by the conquest of the one, so in the end I chose the Tofuku-ji, or Temple of Eastern Happiness, hidden among the smoking pines, maples and cryptomerias of the foothills towards the east.

It is a Zen Buddhist temple and one of the oldest in Japan. Of all the thirty Buddhist sects that have their headquarters in Japan, Zen seemed to me to have the most immediate bearing on the desperate present in Japan and to be of the greatest significance for the future. I say this because Zen is the only branch of Buddhism in Japan which has devoted itself to resolving the clash of fearful opposites in the national soul. I have mentioned these terrible contradictions before, and no one who has read Japanese history and remembers the last war can be unaware of the extent and gravity of the national paradox. At the same

time it is only fair to remember that it is not only a Japanese but a world paradox. It is this clash of opposites in human nature which has made Europe one
of the bloodiest battlegrounds in the history of man; it has made the Germany
of Goethe, Bach and Kant also the Germany of Hitler and Goebbels and has
inflicted even upon a nation of feeling and sensibility like Italy the hubris of
Fascism. Indeed, I believe this clash of opposites presents the oldest challenge
in life to the spirit of man. Long before the birth of Christ the saintly sages of
China dedicated their lives to Tao, which they believed would transform the
clash of the opposites into a union of creative energies. In the twelfth century,
when the national paradox had Japan by the throat, Zen came into being precisely in order to attempt this. In the process it had the most far-reaching effect
on every aspect of the life of Japan and to this day has perhaps the greatest
following of any Buddhist sect in Japan, since of the country's forty-three million Buddhists, ten million adhere to the three main branches of Zen. One
reason for Zen's sustained success in Japan is its contempt for purely intellectual
solutions. Up to the moment of its arrival in Japan, Buddhism had been an
affair of scholars, aristocrats, priests and metaphysicians, whom the masses were
expected obediently to follow. As a result it had become embedded in layer
upon layer of petrifying casuistry. Zen without hesitation turned its back on all
that. Zen was and is not knowledge, theology, or system, but inspired experience. Like the New Testament it speaks to man in parables and is concerned
more with example than with preaching. Briefly, I would say it is dedicated to
the wholeness of man. It aims at making man whole and immediate and it re-
stores to him the validity of his own experience and responsibility alone in the
face of the universe. It abhorred perfection as another way of denying life; it re-
nounced the obsessions of its day with balance and symmetry of forms as a trap
to prevent the spirit from moving on. It believed in a conception of dynamic,
of asymmetry. In Tokyo a young Zen Buddhist monk said to me, "You know,
we have biology on our side. One of the most dynamic innovations in the
history of life was asymmetrical: the placing of the heart not in the middle
of the human body but well on the left side." Above all Zen makes manifest

Page 121 Traditional Kyoto geisha, Takeha Fujimoto, stops outside her home; 122 Yanagizaki Teruo, a Shinto priest, sits in the Heian Shrine; 123 Yano Kushu, a priest in the Nazenji Temple; 124–125 Palanquin bearers rest from their burden at a Kyoto festival; 126 A monk rakes the sand in a Zen garden; 127 Horsemen dismount after one of the numerous historical processions in Kyoto; 128 Apprentices departing for an evening's work in the geisha quarter of Kyoto.

the importance of living life not by rule, but simply and with an heroic self-discipline, by instinct, in the closest possible communion with nature and the universe. It conceives of life as an art rather than a science. As the great interpreter of Zen, Dr. Suzuki, once told me, "Our personal lives are the brush with which we paint our picture on the scroll of history."

As a final example of how the spirit of Zen was transmitted, here is one of my favourite stories. Two Zen monks were walking in the country after a flood. They came to a place where the road was cut by a torrent and the bridge washed away. On the far side a girl in distress called out to the monks, begging them to help her across. Monk A immediately, Zenlike, rolled up his sleeves, girded up his kimono, waded across, put the girl on his shoulder, carried her over the torrent and put her down. Then he and Monk B crossed over themselves and continued on their way. For the first seven miles, however, Monk B, who had done nothing, was deep in thought and silent. Suddenly he said, "Brother, I am very worried. We are holy men and today you have broken your vows by touching a woman and carrying her on your shoulder."

In a flash Monk A replied, "Brother, I saw a human being in need and did what was necessary. When I had carried the girl over the stream, I had done with her and could put her down. But look at you! You have carried her for seven miles!"

To the ordinary people of Japan, the effect of a monastic order deeply engaged in the act of living was tremendous. As a result, after the coming of Zen not one aspect of life in Japan was ever the same again. It laid its revitalising grasp on everything and transformed architecture, poetry, painting, evolved its own kind of landscape gardening as well as creating new forms of expression like the tea ceremony, the *haiku,* and the art of flower arrangement, which to this day are essential ingredients of the life of the land. Even archery was transformed from a mere exercise into a means of living the symbolic life of the spirit. All these considerations inevitably led me to the temple Tofuku-ji.

As I passed through its curved Sammon, the two-storeyed gate which was made in the thirteenth century and sat with heavy grace on its columns, it was as if I had entered into another dimension of reality. After the noise, crowds and the hustle in the more ostentatious temples of the city the stillness was almost absolute. A fitful air played with the exquisite leaves of maples, which stood in the grounds and fluttered in the mist with an odd moth-wing sound in the still air.

The grounds themselves were immense. I had expected to find a temple but instead found a monastic village with more than one sacred building. Behind the main hall which faced us was a deep cleft wherein a mountain stream maintained a soft *shaku-hachi*, bamboo-flute-like note. At the side of some moss-covered steps rising out of the cleft was a long grey stone, rather like those seen in graveyards in England. Carved deeply in Chinese characters on it was Bashō's most famous *haiku*:

Furu-ike ya	An ancient pond:
Kawazu tobikomu	A frog plunges,
Mizu no oto	Then sound of water.

The great vagabond poet of Japan had been enraptured by the condensed form of poetry evolved out of the passion of Zen for the quintessence and its abhorrence of any fatty tissues around the heroic heart.

Beyond the grey stone on a swift rise of ground were more great buildings. They, too, were of wood and had such a close affinity with the earth and the trees that they might have grown out of it. Their grace and beauty were breathtaking. It was beauty beneath the skin. The curved roofs rested on great unstained columns of wood, each carved out of a single primeval tree to reveal the loveliness beneath the bark as round and smooth as any marble column of Greece. The causeways between the buildings, the verandahs and balconies were all of unstained wood. The walls, too, were of wood, the divisions and partitions inside of translucent golden paper or screens painted in colours that glowed rather than burned in the brown of the tranquil recesses. The floors were covered in specially thick mats of beautifully woven and plaited straw.

Each room had its meaning. In one a man could pray alone, in another he brought offerings to an altar at the feet of a golden Buddha, in another he came for sermons or to consult a priest and talk about the abiding meaning of things.

Inevitably this world of wood and paper had been destroyed by fire in the course of the temple's long history. That worried me far more than it did my companions, and I suspected the cause of the difference to be so fundamental that I was not content until I knew the explanation. Under the impulse inherited from Egypt, Greece and Rome, we in Europe build on the presumption that we can defeat time. The Japanese have no such presumption. They live in a land where earthquake, wind, flood and fire repeatedly wreck the staunchest city and temple, and have made a mockery of such ambition. It is not that they are without immortal ambitions. They have different concepts of how to achieve them. They believe that only through undismayed renewal can brittle flesh and blood achieve immortality, and this belief is immeasurably encouraged by the Buddhist doctrine of reincarnation. Thus fire and disaster hurt them less than they hurt us. Indeed, it is almost as if their spirit welcomes these disasters as an opportunity for renewing themselves, their buildings and their institutions.

As a result, one of the most striking things about a country with so old and rich a culture is that it is completely without ancient ruins. A building destroyed is instantly rebuilt if it is thought worth it. The Golden Pavilion of Kyoto, burned down in 1950, today is fully rebuilt and its burnished image burns as bright as it ever did in the blue water at its feet. But if the building is not thought important the remains swiftly vanish.

Therefore one looks in vain in Japan for the equivalents of the broken columns, the crumbling castle walls which flank the roads of history from Egypt to Constantinople, from Athens to Rome and Carcassonne to Salamanca. These buildings in the temple grounds of Tofuku-ji Temple had been reverently renewed, all except the famous rainbow bridge and tower which had been destroyed by a flood some years before. I asked a monk the reason for this and he said the temple had not yet been able to raise the money; the new Japan was not as interested in Zen as before. It was experiencing the same indifferences and lack of popular support as the Christian churches. He went on to say that we were living in a sunset hour of the spirit, but that made Zen all the more important. These things could not be judged by the number of adherents but only by the quality of those who practised them. Never had the quality of the adherents been more truly dedicated. Perhaps the future spirit of Japan, when it has accomplished the immense process of readaptation to a modern technological world which now absorbs its image and imagination, will turn again to the temples for revaluation, as it did before and after the disasters of the twelfth century.

In this way I came to the temple gardens, but they were so unlike my conception of a garden that for a moment I had a deep sense of shock. This was not surprising, as Zen, to use our modern idiom, was from the start a form of shock therapy of the spirit. It aimed at shaking men out of their intellectual pretensions and challenging their imaginations. The garden did something of this sort to me. Nothing grew in it except a little moss. It consisted of fine river gravel raked between low rectangular walls into a series of parallel lines, straight at first but resolving into a series of loops. Near the loops were stones also from a river bed; they were of various sizes and so spaced that they appeared to have a meaningful relationship with one another.

I knew of course that all this was deliberate and typically Zen. Until the Zen masters took Japanese gardening in hand the garden had either been a setting in which to sip green tea in green shade, to hear the songs of the nightingale and the cuckoo, or admire the August moon rocked in the ripples of a pond. But Zen, in its search for the eternal essences, rejected all that. It fashioned gardens only of moss, gravel and stones, since what could represent the river of life more adequately than rocks and gravel fashioned by great waters? Unpromising as this Spartan approach may sound to us, I can only say that I found these two bare gardens, particularly in that rich setting of wisteria and azalea in full bloom, greatly moving. Climbing down into the cleft, I came to the other half of the temple and yet another garden.

Here, in the innermost part of the temple grounds, I had a second surprise. This inner garden was bigger than the first and enclosed on three sides by low monastic buildings. One half of the garden was river gravel raked in the same rows, ripples and whirlpools as the first to express the abiding rhythms of life. But there were no rocks among them. The other half was a garden of stone, grass, shrubs and even some carefully chosen flowers. Down the middle from the modest gate in the wall to the centre of the temple building ran a path made of smooth round cobblestones.

I knew in a flash that I was experiencing a Zen Buddhist symbol of wholeness, an expression of the reconciliation of man's great contradictions. On one side the desert, wherein life must be tested; on the other the earth, the world wherein it must be lived, while the path in front of me was the image of the way to such wholeness. Of course I had a long and animated discussion about this with the monks of the monastery.

After the temple and the gardens came the festival. Near the temples of the centre, Kyoto was crowded with people gathered to see the Aoi Matsuri or Hollyhock Festival. No people in the world are more festive-minded than the Japanese. With a mythology and history reverently remembered, there is not a place in the land without a good excuse to relive some moment of gratitude, of deliverance from disaster, and so it feels the need to appease and have communion with the gods and souls of its illustrious dead.

All year long by the sea, on the mountains, in the rivers and the rice fields, amid snow and ice, in blossoming spring and golden summer, the traveller will suddenly see a procession stitched like French tapestry in brilliant colours in the white, green or grey of the land and hear the sound of the ancient music of a people rededicating themselves to a significant memory. But some of the greatest ceremonies take place in Kyoto.

The Aoi Matsuri is one of these. It is said to have its origin in the sixth century, when the country was overwhelmed with disasters of storms and floods, until finally the gods were pacified by prayer. So on May 15, another grey morning, I watched the procession set out from the old Imperial Palace.

First came a single Suo or forerunner. He was dressed like an early seventeenth-century warrior, and following him through the gate poured the main procession. For three-quarters of an hour it streamed out in ordered symbolic sections: Kado-no-osa, mediaeval police; Kebiishi, officers of police and court administration services; Kajo, courtiers of lowest rank; Yamashiro-Tsukai, the vice-governor of old Kyoto followed by his Eji or soldiers guarding the boxes in which the offerings to the gods are kept; horses in superb trappings to be offered to the gods; the Giisha or Gōshō-Guruam, oxcarts with immense squeaking wheels, carrying impersonators of Emperor and courtiers of highest rank; the Chokushi, the imperial messenger with a sword of gold, mounted on a magnificent bay, followed by his own bodyguard of Zuishin, and after him litters bearing princesses and ladies in waiting, more oxcarts with members of the imperial family, priests, court musicians, more warriors representing all sections of a mediaeval army, young girls leading beflowered oxen by silken cords, young men carrying vast umbrellas—both men and umbrellas decorated with flowers and hollyhock leaves—a palanquin with a woman representing the Emperor's daughter, the Saio or hollyhock maiden of the eighth century, followed by a long suite of more warriors, court ladies, page girls and other members of the feminine mediaeval aristocracy.

I had thought that no one in the world could do court ceremonial as well as the English, but this procession was as moving and colourful as any I had seen. Indeed, the colour and variety of those ancient clothes were unbelievable. They set the grey day on fire and not one section of the procession repeated the colour and uniform of the others.

The attention to detail, too, was amazing. Some of the warriors were dressed in sandals of yellow straw, uniforms of cream and green, and carried long bows of unstained bamboo. Others wore lacquered *geta* and sombre but elegant kimonos, with two swords stuck in the sash. Yet another company came by in scarlet and gold, with vividly lacquered bows and arrows arranged in quivers carried in the middle of the back, like the feathers of a peacock fanned out for display. Still more passed by on horses, bridles decorated with flowers, high wooden saddles ornate with antique colour and great stirrups of vividly lacquered wood. There were priests marching solemnly in gold-and-white robes, others in scarlet capes and black-lacquered hats and mounted on horses. There were young girls, each one a complex painting in many vivid colours, their white porcelain faces made whiter by the long plaits of black hair which fell over their shoulders. Behind them followed beflowered oxen on their leads of silk and yet another great creaking tumbril, decorated with wisteria, iris and plum blossom. Behind the carts came more priests in purple dress, peaked black caps with white cockades. At regular intervals came musicians playing music on antique Japanese harps, flutes and flageolets.

Long after the procession had vanished on its way to the hillside shrines, the music blew like a wind of history among the trees round us. But what impressed me most was the genius of the Japanese to set the appropriate mask on their faces. I had a close, unimpeded view of the procession and I never saw a muscle in a face move, an expression alter, or an eye blink, even the eye of the smallest porcelain maiden, blackbird-bright in her white skin. No one moved out of his inner focus in this sanctified moment of remote history. When the last colour had faded among pines and maples and the music of history was stifled among the leaves, I felt oddly forlorn and the day looked greyer than ever.

I turned then to go back through the garden of the Imperial Palace and at once experienced what I think is one of the most disconcerting aspects of the character of the Japanese: the extraordinary instinct to form crowds. One moment there had been only three of us, the next there appeared to be thirty thousand, churning like a maelstrom round us, all making for the same central exit. The fact that there were other exits was apparently irrelevant.

The physical as well as the emotional pressure of the crowd was frightening. I looked at my Japanese companions, and clearly they had not noticed anything abnormal. I remembered that in 1950 the crowds in Tokyo had rushed to the Imperial Palace to pay their respects to the Emperor in such numbers that scores of them had been stifled or quietly, steadily and gently pressed to death by the weight of such dangerously single-minded humanity. Even the Japanese had been horrified by the deaths and since had taken to queuing for these occasions. But in old-fashioned Kyoto apparently no such idea had yet penetrated the popular mind.

The experience, uncomfortable as it was, would hardly merit recall did I not believe it to represent a formidable national phenomenon: the Japanese seem to find it difficult to experience life individually and in isolation, and this makes them dangerously prone to group tyranny. One of my most vivid memories in a Japanese prison was how when one sentry beat us, the other sentries from all over the camp felt bound to come rushing along to identify themselves with the deed by beating the rest of us as well, so that what would have been one beating quickly became thirty. It is precisely because of this tendency that the pragmatic faith of Zen of Kyoto has laid such emphasis on the responsibility of the individual to himself and his duty to live as one in the company of the many.

The last night in Kyoto we dined in the old city in one of the oldest restaurants in Japan. It had been run by the same family for four hundred years, and the rooms were so small and the ceilings so low that I had to move with care. But the compensations were so many that I soon forgot these limitations. The food, the garden, the service, the lighting to me seemed a perfect end to the Hollyhock Day. Finally there were the geisha, or geikō as they are called in the attractive Kyoto dialect. There were two of them and one maiku or apprentice geisha. They were there largely because of my student companion who had never been to a geisha party before. He said simply that he had never had enough money to treat himself to a geisha party. So I had to guide him through the etiquette that the occasion demanded. We sat in our loose *yukata* on our *zabuton,* relaxed and warm after our bath, eating slowly, while the three young ladies kept us entertained with bright conversation, quips and sallies. When the meal was over the maiku danced a dance called "Spring Rain." She danced it as centuries of geisha had danced it before her, not only with her body but through the movement of her head, the gestures of her hand, the noise of the wind in the swish of her flamboyant kimono and the crash of thunder in the fall of her fan to the floor. When the gestures failed, the music took over. But now the two geisha demanded that we should "chiku-dansu," i.e., dance cheek to cheek with them. We had no option but to do this, awkwardly in rooms too small and cramped for such a day and age, while the maiku at the samisen sang a song which I can only roughly translate to this effect:

> This afternoon
> In your baseball match,
> The umpire counted:
> One two three, one two three,
> One two three,
> And thrice you were out
> But when we dance
> Cheek to cheek in each other's arms
> We are in the world
> Where no umpire
> Except death can call us out.

Thereafter we sat down again to talk. My companion asked question after question of one geisha about her life. Nothing made her so indignant, our informant told us, as the popular Western belief that the geisha were just superior prostitutes. They were women of great intelligence and accomplishment, with their own great *amour-propre* and sense of integrity. It is true, as Japanese literature showed, that they had been mistresses and lovers of many eminent men, and as such exercised considerable influence on historic affairs. But also they had followed their hearts and loved hopelessly penniless students, artists and others. They had profound loyalties and values of their own. Only a fool would treat them lightly. To this day friendship with an eminent geisha could make a man's career as much as the devotion of a suitable wife. In fact geisha made notoriously good wives, and exemplary priestesses and nuns. All this I heard the geisha tell my companion, but he was beyond the point where generalities would satisfy him.

"But how did *you* become a geisha?" he asked the slim, dark-eyed girl.

Her parents were poor so they had sold her on contract for ten years to a Mama-San, or Mrs. Mother. This Mrs. Mother sent her to the geisha school in Kyoto for three years, where as well as continuing her ordinary tuition, she studied music, poetry, singing, dancing, literature, the art of conversation, acting and even some English. Then she had gone out to practise in the world what she had learned at school. The Mrs. Mother usually had three or four geisha who lived with her, and since she was poor too, she usually had a financial arrangement with some of the honourable teahouses. We could have no idea how expensive were a geisha's training and dressing. She herself at that moment had on clothes that cost $1500, and a famous geisha's wardrobe could easily run to $15,000 and more. Neither Mrs. Teahouse nor Mrs. Mother could combine to raise so vast a sum, and in order to do so a geisha would need a Mr. Father. Yes—she nodded her head—a geisha needed a kind, rich gentleman who would take the geisha under his protection and to whom she would give all her loyalty in return.

This depressed my companion and he protested, "Surely that is not what you want?"

She looked at him with a compassion too old for her years and said gently, "If a good, kind man came and offered me his protection now and in my old age, I would be very happy. It is true we have now formed a geisha's trade union and have negotiated wage agreements with provisions for pensions, but I would prefer a decent protector."

He shook his head and exclaimed angrily, "I do not understand!"

"There are some things better not understood," she answered, uttering the death sentence of the party as far as he was concerned. Later she asked me if we could drop them on our way to our own inn. While he telephoned for a taxi, the geisha went to change. When they returned I hardly recognised them.

The piles of hair we had admired so much had been wigs. They stood before us with shingled hair. Quickly a taxi took us to the geisha quarter. The reflection of paper lanterns and rooms of amber behind paper screens sparkled in the waters of the river. The street was warm and glowing with light and bright with geisha and maiku on lacquered *geta,* karo-koro-ing, karo-koro-ing in and out of narrow alleyways. There, indeed, existed a Japan that was a thousand years old. The taxi stopped outside a neat teahouse from which the sound of more nostalgic samisen music came. The three girls got out.

"Please, may I come with you?" my companion asked his favourite.

"You do me a great honour," she said, bowing low and hissing between her teeth, "and I thank you humbly, but I fear since you have not been introduced to Mrs. Teahouse and Mrs. Mother it would not be permitted. Please be so good as to come back and arrange to be introduced at some other honourable moment." She bowed again and vanished through a translucent doorway.

VI

The Body of Japan

After Kyoto we went to Nara, where we stopped briefly since the two are in a sense continuations of each other. Nara began what Kyoto so triumphantly completed. For seventy-four years it was the capital of Japan and the centre of an astonishing renaissance. The renaissance came as the result of a stand against the fear of death in the Japanese spirit. Until Nara was founded, for thousands of years the Japanese had moved their capital to a new site every time an emperor died. But at Nara, probably because of the impact of Buddhism and its doctrine of eternal renewal, the Japanese found the courage to face and take up the dark challenge evaded for so long. How great had been their fear can perhaps be measured best today by contemplating the size of one of the first statues of Buddha raised in Nara. It is over fifty feet high, and more than five hundred tons of brass and lead and zinc were used in casting it, I was told. The Todai-ji, or Great Eastern Temple, which was built to house it, though only a fraction of its original size, is still the greatest wooden building in the world, just as the Buddha remains the greatest bronze statue. All this was accomplished in the eighth century. Today Nara is much smaller than its original self, but the buildings that remain are the oldest wooden buildings in the world and house some of the oldest and most beautiful works of man.

Walking by the quiet waters in the Nara parks, feeding the deer that beg

Page 145 Men of Nikko dressed as soldiers of the early Tokugawan Shogunate; 146 A woman walks her dog through the courtyard of the shrine in Asaksa; 147 The chief priest of the Heian Shrine in Kyoto rides in a carriage during a parade; 148–149 The peak of the Quarrel Festival in Himeji; 150 A street in Asaksa, the entertainment centre for provincial visitors to Tokyo; 151 Women shoppers stop to talk in a mountain village; 152–153 The wheat fields of Shikoku Island; 154 A music shop in the Shinjuku area of Tokyo; 155 A dance-hall hostess watches for prospective customers; 156–157 An official of the shrine at Nikko, resting before a display of saki hampers; 158 Fishermen bringing in the nets full of bream, near Tomo; 159 Rice planters at work near Nigata; 160 Two ladies bid farewell in an old section of the city of Takayama.

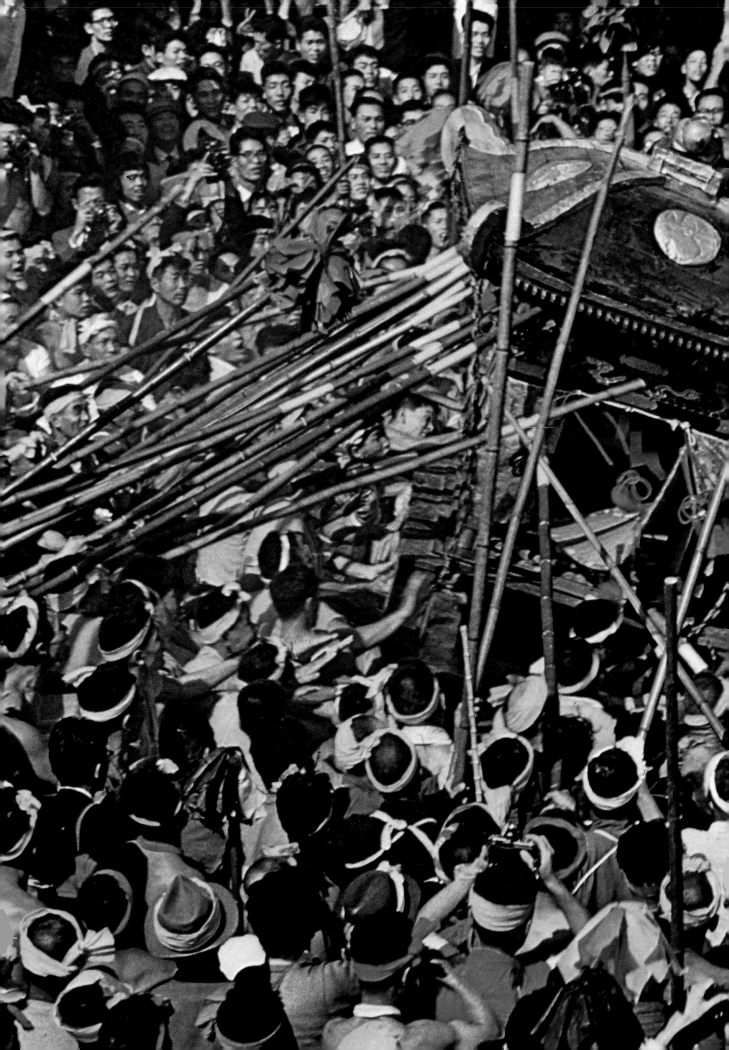

for food among the multitudes, entering the Shinto shrine and then the inner-most hall of a temple to stand before a golden Buddha, one is made aware of how dynamically the Japanese sense of communion with nature was joined to a Buddhist awareness of the more conscious claims of life and the necessity for enlightenment of the instinctive and intuitive in man.

At Nara, at last, the sun came out and from there on the country of Japan was seen in a light trembling with the magic of spring. That light in Japan has to be experienced to be believed. Over the seasons it can have as many contradictions as the national character. In winter the winds from Sakhalin and Kamchatka either blur it with snow or freeze it into an arctic clarity. But in spring and early summer the south wind fills it with the warmth and humidity of the tropics until the heavens hang glowing like one vast raindrop between one's eyes and the sun. There is no other light in the world quite so charged with atmosphere. As a result distances seem greater and the moon seems to swing farther into the sky at night than elsewhere.

I watched one of the lovely five-storeyed pagodas of this city gathering the light to it. The pagoda is to the Japanese scene what the church spire is to the English. In the land there are pagodas as high as five stories swaying flowerlike on their tall, slender stalks of bamboo, expressing the same abiding aspiration to higher things as Gothic steeples.

Instead of crosses, there are always the wooden torii, the sacred gateways to the innumerable shrines of the land. Sometimes the torii are just two simple upright wooden columns holding a single cross beam over a pathway leading to a small unadorned wooden shrine hidden among cypresses and cedars. Or they can be more elaborate, occasionally lacquered a bright red, but in whatever shape or form, there is hardly a valley, mountain, or plain without one or more in view.

So they have stood for some thousands of years, emerging from the depths of the national soul. They are indeed the supreme image of the indigenous way to Shinto which, as the name so clearly states, is the way of the gods. Even the ancient name of the Japanese for their emperor, the Mikado, reveals something of the profundity of the image of the torii, since it means nothing more or less than "the August gate."

Few nations have a history so old, long-sustained and uninterrupted as the Japanese; but in terms of geological time, their land is young. The earth has still a gloss upon it like the sheen on a newborn calf—which one does not find in the really ancient lands like Australia and Africa. The mountains and hills rise steeply out of the plain with all the impetuousness of the original impulse. Time and weather so far have made little impression on them. They remain unblurred and their outlines are clean and clear like the blades of a spear, giving the wider scenes an Euclidian precision that one sees in the classic woodcuts of Japan.

Much of the country is still under its aboriginal cover of trees. Forests sweep over the hilltops in their primeval abundance, march down to the edge of lake, stream and sea and at sunset burn like torches on the precise skylines. The varieties of trees seem endless: pines, giant cryptomeria, cypress, oak, maple, camphor-laurel, birch, beech, larch, fir, palmetto, more than fifty kinds of bamboo, and many another species from tropical to sub-arctic grow side by side in the same ardent, young soil. Each species adds its own quality to the rich scene and has its own moment of glory: the maple on fire in the autumn; the cherry and plum in spring; the cryptomeria darkly monumental all the year round along the formal avenues of pomp and circumstance leading to the lacquered tomb; the pines twisted and tenacious, manning the steepest slopes and sheltering the most difficult earth, and the bamboo like feathered arrows gracing gardens, fields, humps and hilltops in quiverfuls.

Among these hills, superbly clothed in this manner, flow the great crystal rivers, streams and brooks. Sometimes they form lakes as at Chuzenji, where the deep water is so still and clear that rowing over it I have seen the shadow of my boat following like a cloud on the very bottom of the lake. Often they fall abysmally over cliffs but in the fall assume shapes and patterns that one sees nowhere else. There are no Niagaras or Victorias in Japan, but there are falls like the Kegon descending from a great height into a volcanic abyss, slender, platinum and snow-white, with all the delicacy and lightness of a bridal veil. At the foot of the fall its waters join the river in the Nikko Valley, where shrines and tombs in blazing colours flicker among the sombre masses of giant trees, and all together they stream triumphantly out of a narrow black pass under the single, graceful arch of a bridge of lacquered vermilion, and so out to sea.

No wonder that this indigenous beauty has so great a hold on the imagination. It moves people to profound reverence and high poetic exaltation, and it provokes in them dangerous dissatisfaction with the ugliness of the battle for existence and the imperfections of life on earth. Thus there is hardly a place of beauty that does not encourage the abnormal tendency to suicide that I have mentioned. The Kegon waterfall, for instance, is one of the favourite places for double suicides of despairing young couples in love. They write tender verses of farewell to life, or merely a *"gomen nasai,"* or "forgive us, please," with their names on a piece of rice paper and pin it to a tree nearby, before they hurl themselves over the falls into the delicate waters below.

Beneath it all the earth of Japan is thin-skinned and unduly sensitive. The fires of the world burn fiercely within, close to the surface. The terrifyingly high earthquake rate reminds one of this fact, and hardly a district is without its hot springs and geysers gushing out of the earth, reeking of brimstone and sulphur. There are large .areas from Beppu in the south to Noboribetsu in the north where the earth so bubbles and hisses with volcanic water and steam that the air smells like rotting cabbage.

There are at Beppu alone many *jigoku,* or ponds, over four hundred feet deep where the hidden fires and hot waters of the land have made a porridge of the earth, boiling it so furiously that the bubbles hurl the gruel many feet into the air. On those still days of spring and early summer you are continuously aware of a fearful fever in the earth; its pulse beat seems faster than in any other volcanic land, and this rapid, violent heartbeat imparts a steady vibration to the scene, so that everything is faintly shivering and even the translucent air trembles like liquid ether.

I felt this everywhere but nowhere more than in Kyushu, the great south island of Japan. There the fire and the fever in the earth seemed to affect everything. Vegetation grows at double the normal rate. I saw on one and the same day the farmers harvesting wheat next to fields wherein oats and barley stood shoulder-high, while below in the water-filled paddies, blue with reflected sky, their women were busy planting the rice they harvested twice a year. Above them on the higher slopes trees were already heavy with plums, apricots, apples, persimmons; and dark-green tea bushes in long regular rows were waiting to be picked. All the time the shining air around vibrated in one's ears like the sound of a high-powered car. This sound was magnified by the noise of the millions of cicada singing of earthquake and eruption among the trees. When my Japanese friends first heard it with me in Kyushu, they became wildly excited and insisted on finding a tree away from roads and noise under which they could enjoy the sound. They told me they could distinguish five kinds of cicada, but bass or soprano, they all sang for me the song of the passionate fires concealed in that green, tender and eager earth.

One day, as if to confirm the authenticity of the cicada song, there came our first earthquake. It was slight and without danger but swept like a tidal wave over the bright ripples of cicada song. On that day at noon in the provincial capital, Kumamoto, I was in a bank cashing a traveler's cheque when the floor beneath my feet and the concrete walls around me began to shake like jelly. The Japanese cashier went on calmly writing a voucher for me as if he had not felt the sinister movement.

"But surely this is an earthquake!" I exclaimed.

"Yes, of course!" he answered without looking up.

Finally there is supreme reminder in the great volcano Mt. Aso, also a favourite exit from life of lovers in despair. Around it there are no trees, only bare slopes of grass and a cone in the blue wherein a long feather of smoke stands like the quill of a pen which writes not with ink but lava.

The people of Kyushu have deep in their character something of the fierce abundance of energy and the extremes of passive acceptance and violent rebellion of their native earth. Elsewhere the differences between the peoples of the main islands are not great. A remarkably long history and culture have seen to that. But the men and women of Kyushu seem to possess a quality which can perhaps be best summed up in the Japanese phrase *Jo-netsu-teki:* a passionate and inflammable spirit. As a result they have had an influence on the history of Japan out of all proportion to their numbers.

On such a dynamic earth, in so volcanic and yet primeval a setting, the Japanese countryman builds his farms and villages with a remarkable absence of the dramatic. His farms and villages of wood and paper so belong to the earth that they look as if they have grown out of it. The sense of belonging between people and earth is stupendous. Among the purple shadows, a village often merges so well with the background that one can scarcely detect it. The humble country buildings are of impeccable proportions and workmanship. Outwardly to the European eye the lack of paint and the austere simplicity may at first seem drab. Only when you look deeper into the workmanship, the material and the underlying conception, you discover a beauty of bone beneath the skin.

Despite the uniformity of style, each farm and village seems to have its own mysterious recipe for existence. This is partly due to the nature of the manifold earth which does not allow you to see the land in grand vistas; the valleys and plains are, on the whole, small and separated from one another by the sharp, clear dividing lines of precise hills. But when you do encounter a variation of colour or building it has an intoxicating effect. Sometimes the colour is in the spectacle of ancient pageantry on its way to a country shrine, or from rolls of cloth laid out on a river bank to dry after the process of dyeing, or merely from the magnificent kimonos of a trio of maiku climbing up the grey steps of a brown temple. Always the wild flowers are unforgettable. In autumn there are the maples, in spring cherry and plum blossom, and the whole countryside is set on fire. But all the year round there is colour in the lacquer in the building of temple, tomb and shrine. At Itsukushima, at the end of a grey village hemmed in between the steep forest-covered slopes and the sea, you suddenly see some immense curved thatched roofs among dark-green pines and grey stone walls, and below the thatch there flashes the red of the lacquered eaves and round pillars and the madonna-blue of the boarding on the verandahs. When the tide flows in through the sacred gate, which stands on yellow sand, it swirls as blue as heaven beneath the arches of a wooden bridge with red-lacquer railings and continues on to wash freely around the vermilion base of the shrine itself. Sometimes, too, green and gold boats ride on the tide, sail in through the gate and up to the inmost shrine.

Occasionally, too, you come across a castle. Then you are amazed that the Japanese can build so enduringly in stone. Those curved walls stand out with majestic decision above the blue waters of their wide moats. One in particular remains in my mind: Himeji, or the Castle of the White Heron. There are other greater castles that have been rebuilt after destruction in the last or other wars, but this one survives in its original shape. The massive walls when I saw them were yellow in the light, the moat was blue, and above the stone of the balustrades rose a long, delicate wall of white topped with the mauve tiles of a curved roof. Beyond the walls soared the slanted walls of stone of the inner keep, rising to more walls of white and tiers of mauve roofs, culminating in a single turret of great height, where only the white heron could safely roost. It looked a very refuge and fortress in time of trouble. But above and beyond all buildings were the neat fields of the gleaming plains, the stacked terraces of small enclosed valleys ending abruptly against the angled slopes of the triangular hill.

Only in the far north, in Hokkaido, is there the suggestion of a new note. The proximity of the Arctic, the cold north winds, the frost and the ice have given the vegetation there a fine-drawn look that you don't see in the south. The houses are sturdier, and delicate silver birch and fir rather than Japanese cypress and bamboo grace the earth. The people have a sturdy, oddly Finnish look; the farms, a strangely Scandinavian appearance. The climate and the long dark winter perhaps explain why no farmhouse or village dwelling is without a television antenna.

Yet it would be a grave mistake to imagine that even so severe and long a winter has cooled the fires burning in such passionate earth. No snow and ice have yet quenched the fires of volcanoes like Akan, Tokachi-dake, Daisetsu-zan and Tarumai, and at places like Noboribetsu in the dead of winter you can stand on your skis on the edge of the Jigoku-dani, or Valley of Hell, watching the earth hissing steam, sulphur and boiling water and spurting high the bubbling porridge of mud. One hot spring is still used as a village kitchen and the people boil their chickens and vegetables daily in its waters.

In the far north, too, the disaster of earthquake, fire, wind, flood and tidal wave always threatens. I myself experienced no earthquake, but I crossed the strait between the main island and Hokkaido a bare half-hour before a tidal wave, coming from the Pacific waters of South America, swept over it and drowned hundreds of persons.

But even in the deepest and most traditional parts of the deep countryside the twentieth century intrudes, continually reminding one how irrevocably Japan is committed to change. These intrusions are less dramatic than in the towns but somehow far more startling. For instance, I was at Gifu for the opening night of the cormorant fishing, which the aristocracy of Japan have loved to watch ever since the eighth century. In the dark I went out to the fishing grounds in a long wooden boat with a turned-up nose and a crew of two soft-spoken boatmen who told me the history of cormorant fishing and explained the technicalities. We arrived at our station to find the dark waters of the river bright with the light of paper lanterns of many other boats. I was the only foreigner there and my boat was austere compared to the rest, for all the others had geisha and maiku in them for every male spectator.

They sang, talked and laughed until suddenly round a bend appeared a large flat-bottomed boat looking like a floating pavilion decorated with garlands of flowers. The interior was lit with lanterns and in it stood ten young ladies of the best Gifu families, bowing to us in bright kimonos. They sang, danced and played their guitars for us, while four boatmen poled them up and down the long line of spectators. Their songs praised the cormorant fishing and fishermen of Gifu, of course, but the last verses invariably could not resist comparing the light of the fishermen's boat, the art of fishing and its successes and disappointments with the course of human love. One song, braver than the rest, I remember, ended with the positive conclusion: "Nonetheless let us follow the fire of our love into the night, as the fishermen follows the fire in the bow of his ship in the dark, and so find each other as he finds fish in the waters of the flowing river."

Whenever the sounds of their young voices died away there was a moment of silence and one heard only the river and, from the steep volcanic hill behind, the bright chatter of thousands of crickets in the forest. It was all very beautiful and truly out of another day and civilisation. When at last the fishermen appeared with a great fire dangling in the iron basket in the bow of each boat, the boat of girls, flowers and music discreetly withdrew. For some two hours the fishermen fished with their cormorants in the waters round us, the master in each boat plying eight birds on silk reins, his assistant four, while another steered the boat and a fourth fed the fire. The fire drew the fish to the boats and the excited cormorants could not dive after them fast enough. They splashed and darted about and a murmur of applause broke from the excited spectators as bird after bird was hauled in to give up the silver fish in its gullet. The sight of man, beast and bird combining for a mutual end has always moved me, but never more so than by paper-lantern light on that dark, wide river, where it had a quality of the original magic of life about it.

I could have watched it all night, but suddenly above the clear line of the hill a great moon appeared, so bright that it eclipsed the fishermen's fires. Instantly the sport was over and our revels ended. As my boat turned home to the inn, a loudspeaker in the primeval wood on the side of the moon-flooded hill gave forth the song, not of Gifu women, but of an ancient record of Sir Harry Lauder singing "Annie Laurie," followed by a modern rendering of "Auld Lang Syne."

Ah, that "Auld Lang Syne" of Burns! I was to come across it over and over again in Japan. Every time my ship went out of a harbour on the Inland Sea, a radio or a band played it for us. It has become the musical farewell of Japan, the sayonara, that "if-it-must-be-so" which for long served as the only appropriate good-bye for a people so full of the uncertainty of human fate. At Misumi in Kyushu I saw even a band of Japanese schoolgirls in tartans and tam-o'-shanters playing a shipful of schoolboys out to sea to the tune of Burns's song and in the process giving it a vital, volcanic urge and violence.

Back in Hokkaido I went to look at an Ainu village, eager to see what was left of the Ebishi, the barbarians who had fought so long, hard and vainly against the Japanese. I went in a crowded bus, a little Japanese boy on my knee, who whenever he was restless was rebuked by his mother with the words: "Please keep still, Mr. Little Boy."

We all bundled out of the bus in the village and were greeted by a squat bearded man followed by a bearded woman, both dressed in short gowns with black-and-blue checks, their legs covered by cross-strapped woolen gaiters.

The Japanese bowed to them politely and said in one voice, "Good day, Mr. and Mrs. Aborigine."

Mr. Aborigine showed us his wood, straw and grass hut, his family heirlooms and the wooden statues he had carved of the bear which is indigenous to his land and the supreme totem of his tribe. We all paid him well for the privilege.

After the Japanese left I stayed behind to wait for a train. Once the tourists had gone I was amazed to see Mr. Aborigine reappear in European clothes and vanish into a neat two-storey house with a tall television aerial over it. "Whose house is that?" I asked a shopkeeper.

"Oh, that," he answered with a marked note of envy, "that is the honourable house of Mr. Aborigine."

Just before I arrived at Noboribetsu in Hokkaido, a young Japanese couple thought to have been hopelessly in love had thrown themselves into a crater of boiling mud. A brilliant young Japanese television engineer who was with me and the Miss Waitress from the inn insisted on taking me to the scene. Crowds of Japanese dressed in the *yukata* and kimono supplied by the inns were wandering in and out of clouds of steam and hissing sulphur like ghosts

169

out of the past. Some were listening to a guide's detailed account of the suicide, which ended with the remark that it was an extremely painful way out since it took a person six minutes to die.

"Did they not leave a message of farewell?" someone asked him.

"No, nothing at all," the guide answered, oddly apologetic.

A hiss of astonishment broke from his audience and one woman exclaimed, "Oh, how pitiful!"

I was not sure whether it was the suicide itself that was pitiful or the breach of suicide etiquette in not leaving behind a poem or some other expression of motive and contrition. I knew only that the thought of two young people being driven to end their lives that way depressed me profoundly. Why, I asked my companions, was there so much suicide in Japan? Was it because their imagination fundamentally was more attracted by tragedy than happiness and found death more romantic than life? Miss Waitress thought that suicides were "cannot-be-helped things" and added, "Sooner or later the world betrays all of us."

The television engineer stared at her with admiration before asking me if I had ever heard of the term *mono-no-aware,* signifying the awareness in the Japanese spirit of the transience of things and the belief that they must be accepted? Suicide was the dark aspect of *mono-no-aware,* but unfortunately it had a bright side: it taught the Japanese obedience to the laws of nature, made them modest and joined people in a common sense of sympathetic sadness. Allied to it was a concept he called *furyū,* which meant a state of mind dedicated to communion with all that was beautiful and creative in nature. No one would understand the Japanese, he claimed, who did not understand the depth of their *mono-no-aware* feelings and *furyū* state of mind. Television, war, washing machines, democracy had not altered them at all in these respects.

Later, while we drank cups of green tea underneath a cherry tree in full bloom, some petals came fluttering down to cover the earth with the first flakes of what the Japanese call "cherry snow."

"Post-san! Look!" The television engineer held out his blue-and-white cup for us to examine.

Miss Waitress and I both looked and saw a single pink cherry petal floating on the pale-green tea.

"Isn't it wonderful?" he said. "There you have *mono-no-aware* and *furyu* in one."

He paused and then said he would like to recite a poem by a man who had been a great mediaeval warrior and who died young in battle. The night before he was killed he wrote:

> Night falls:
> a cherry tree
> is my hospice:
> its flower
> my host.

All the way back to Tokyo it seemed to me that the strength and the weakness in the national character of Japan came out in that brief conversation in the Valley of Hell at Noboribetsu. There is so much of the "it-can't-be-helped" attitude. It may be true, as Miss Waitress said, that the world betrays us all. But I suspect that until the Japanese acquire in great measure the sense of responsibility for the daily betrayal of life that all men share, as well as the capacity of the individual to influence this responsibility, they will not be free of the darker aspects of their history and civilisation.

I was still pondering this when I came to Tokyo. I had been so long with only Japanese that at first I was almost shocked by the Europeans in the lounge of my hotel. I thought I had never seen more hideous people. They looked like caricatures of human beings with everything exaggerated: their noses seemed enormous, their mouths wide and frightening; ears, hands, feet, all too big and cumbersome. Their voices sounded like the crack of doom, and their manners, after those of the quiet, soft-spoken, neat, clean, ever courteous people of Japan, were those of barbarians. But then I caught a reflection of myself in a mirror and, after that, who was I to judge?

A business acquaintance came up to me. "Weren't you frightened out in the country all by yourself?" he asked.

"No," I answered, adding, "I wish I felt as safe in my native South Africa."

"Do you think we are safe tonight?" he asked half-jokingly.

Outside, the demonstrations against the signing of the American treaty and the forthcoming visit of President Eisenhower were in full force. The streets were crowded with protesting people. While I had been in Japan political agitation had grown and I had encountered its ripples in the countryside. There the agitation had taken the form of sober processions of workers from lumber camps, cotton mills and coal mines, marching quietly up and down with banners covered with slogans. But here in Tokyo it had taken a turn for violence, and many of the Europeans in my hotel were frightened.

I could not accept that such fear was justified and I went out into the streets to see for myself. I was immediately struck by the extreme youth of the demonstrators. Most of the youth of Tokyo seemed committed to the anti-government, anti-American demonstrations. They were all highly organised in companies, each with a man armed with a whistle in charge. As he blew his whistle, so they danced and manoeuvred. All—boys and girls, men and women—had red kerchiefs tied round their heads and red ribbons round their arms. They danced a snake dance, a curious exalted expression on their faces and a tranced look in their eyes like the look I'd seen on the faces of young men carrying a palanquin of their gods to their shrine on a feast day. These young demonstrators were committing themselves with all the ardour that their forefathers had shown for traditional causes.

Watching them, I knew that they had done with resignation to the past. They might not know where they were going, but they were on their own way, and nothing would stop them. It did not matter that I thought they were wrong. Indeed, I told them so, for a company of snake-dancing demonstrators came to a halt where I stood and some of them, taking me for an American, spoke to me, saying, "Please, honourable sir, do not imagine there is anything personal in this. It is only that we feel forced to disagree with your policy. Do you not think we have a right to go our own way?"

Before I could answer the whistle blew and obediently my questioners started jogging their fantastic palanquin step-dance again, but not before a girl and a student had caught me by the arm and laughingly carried me along.

Later the scenes became more violent, and the conflict clearly became one of Japanese against Japanese: the new and old in the nation. I was astounded then not so much by the violence as by the behaviour of the Japanese police.

Before the war they were arrogant and ruthless. Now they seemed powerless before the mob. I think that since the war the sinfulness of violence and force has been drummed into the people so deeply that those in authority can no longer employ it even to curb the violence of a revolt.

I have no doubt that the change in the Japanese is sincere, but into what they have changed not even they themselves know. The least intellectual and rational of peoples, a unique race guided more by the heart than by the head, and with all manner of complex and hypersensitive feelings, they tend not to know what they are going to do until they have done it. They need for that reason a far more complex and imaginative understanding and approach than we have been able to give them in the past. I consider them to be a nation of great and unique quality, and the demands they make on our imagination and under-standing, if we meet them halfway, will enrich us as much as them. Particularly the young, in their rejection of the negations of their past and in their indis-criminate hunger for the great wide world of today, are following the authentic prompting and highest presentiment of the national spirit.

Finally there came the moment of my going. I had arrived in Japan at night. I left it at night. As my plane soared out of the murk over the capital, there was Fujiyama as if it had never known cloud but only snow, and above it the full moon. The mountain and the moon seemed heaven-sent images of what is most enduring in Japan: Fujiyama, the perfect rounded mountain shape, the hill of hills for a people to lift eyes to for help, the image of the search of the

Japanese for beauty and proportion, indeed for a life that would deliver them from the bondage of terrible extremes; and as long as Fujiyama stands I believe this great nation will never lack for seekers.

Then the moon—ah, yes, that magnified, almost over-life-size moon of Japan, the image of the spirit of renewal of the Japanese people, a spirit which no cataclysm of water, earth, fire, or wind, nor apocalypse of man has been able to extinguish. Living everywhere as we all do in a sunset hour of time, this image of the moon is one which we, in both the old and the new worlds, could take to heart.

And since then I have been amazed when thinking of Japan, as I do a great deal, how my mind returns to that final vision of the mountain and the moon sinking in a silver sea behind my plane. I know that since I began this book the externals of life in Japan have changed at a great pace. Japan is now committed and mechanically involved in the accelerating technological world of our time. Already she has mastered the industrial idiom of our day so well that in many ways she has begun to lead where once she was forced to imitate blindly or, at best, follow intelligently.

Statistically, the picture is now rather different from the one I give. I would have changed the few statistics I use were it not for two reasons. One: statistics of Japan, even more than those of any other country I know, are out of date before they are compiled. Two, and more important: statistics do not measure the quality and the being of a nation; they measure the quantity, or at best imply certain directions of development. I believe my slight statistical picture is enough to give an idea of the volume and the direction of the evolution of Japan. I myself was and remain far more concerned with the quality and the essence of Japanese life. One of the most common errors of our own time is to attach overmuch importance to externals. Technology, important as it is, makes less difference to the innermost character of people than we care to admit. It gives people new ways and other dimensions of expressing themselves; it does not change their fundamental selves.

I believe this to be more true of Japan than any other country in the world, and for that reason the traditional aspects of the Japanese, their far background and history, which is so old that it is not recorded but manifests itself as a form of national psychology, here remain my chief concern and are most stressed in my interpretation. Other approaches might convey more of what the modern Japanese "has"; this approach I hope indicates more of what she "is." In all the surface paradox of life in Japan this history and background are the source of its inspiration and of the spirit in which it is so deeply rooted: Japan can throw itself wide-open to all the influences and forces of change storming across the modern scene in a way that appears reckless and abandoned, but that makes countries that claim to be in the van of human progress, like Russia, appear as old-fashioned and hesitant as a septuagenarian maiden aunt trapped into witnessing a performance of the Beatles. Japan has the confidence to do this because it knows in its secret heart that its own special roots are sturdy and deep enough to keep it growing and upright, whatever the wind of change blowing through our desperate time.

I could also, of course, have given an example chronologically better than the one I use here of student unrest and political agitation. I rejected the idea because in terms of meaning I would not have gained anything by such a change. Only the night before I wrote these words I saw a long television documentary of student agitation in Japan, particularly against American policy in Vietnam. It was in exactly the same pattern as the demonstration I describe here and reinforced my instinct to leave my illustration intact because it helps to show, in its small way, the continuity of heart and mind underneath the broken surfaces of life.

And now I am back with my last vision of the mountain and the moon.

During the war a book about Japan that rightly had a great influence on American military policy chose as its basic image and title: *The Chrysanthemum and the Sword.* As a seed of thought applied to one mood of one of the most complex people on earth, no image could have served so well at the time. But for a person like myself who has known Japan in three different moments of time, all far apart: as a boy in 1926; a soldier and a prisoner of war seventeen years later; and again in the 'sixties, the last occasion only the other day, I find that the abiding image at the center of all my experience and thinking about Japan is that of the perfect mountain and the full moon as I saw them from my plane.

When I write my book on the three Japans I best know, as I shall have to do, I shall be compelled to call it for that reason "The Mountain and the Moon."